THE MEDIT
DIET CO(
FOR TWO

A Taste of Good Health – Simple and Delicious
Mediterranean Recipes for Couple

Keri Fox

TABLE OF CONTENTS

CHAPTER 6: DESSERTS AND SWEETS FOR TWO 143

CONCLUSION 168

INTRODUCTION

Welcome and Introduction to the Mediterranean Diet

In this cookbook, we embark on a culinary journey through the sun-drenched regions of the Mediterranean, where nourishment isn't just a source of food but a celebration of life itself. Whether cooking for yourself and your partner, a dear friend, or a family member, this cookbook is designed to make your Mediterranean dining experience delightful and healthful.

Why it's Ideal for Couples or Two People

The Mediterranean diet is particularly well-suited for couples or pairs for several reasons. Its core principles align with the notion of sharing and savoring meals together:

1. **Portion Control:** Mediterranean cuisine emphasizes quality over quantity. It encourages you to savor every bite, perfect for couples enjoying delicious meals without overindulging.
2. **Fresh Ingredients:** Many Mediterranean recipes are designed to showcase the freshness of ingredients. For two people, it's easier to procure and enjoy seasonal produce, seafood, and other key components that make Mediterranean cuisine so exceptional.
3. **Social Dining:** Mediterranean eating places importance on communal meals and shared experiences. Cooking and dining together as a couple can strengthen your bond and create memorable moments.

Mediterranean Diet's Principles and Benefits

The Mediterranean diet is a healthy lifestyle rooted in the traditions of Mediterranean countries like Greece, Italy, and Spain. At its core, it emphasizes:

- **Abundance of Fresh Produce:** Fruits, vegetables, whole grains, legumes, and nuts form the foundation of the diet, providing essential vitamins, minerals, and fiber.
- **Healthy Fats:** Olive oil is a staple, providing monounsaturated fats that promote heart health. It's used for cooking and as a dressing.
- **Lean Proteins:** Fish and seafood are favored sources of protein, along with poultry. Red meat is consumed in moderation.
- **Dairy in Moderation:** Yogurt and cheese are enjoyed in moderation, providing calcium and probiotics.
- **Flavorful Herbs and Spices:** Mediterranean cuisine uses herbs and spices like basil, oregano, garlic, and rosemary to add flavor without excessive salt.

- **Wine in Moderation:** Red wine, enjoyed in moderation, may offer heart-healthy benefits when consumed responsibly.

Benefits of the Mediterranean Diet:

- **Heart Health:** Numerous inquiries about ponders have found that taking a Mediterranean slim down can decrease the hazard of heart sickness, lower cholesterol levels, and maintain solid blood weight.
- **Weight Management:** Its focus on whole foods and portion control makes this a great option for controlling your weight and keeping your body in good shape.
- **Longevity:** Regions following the Mediterranean diet have some of the world's highest life expectancies, partly attributed to dietary habits.
- **Improved Cognitive Health:** Some research suggests that the Mediterranean diet could help protect our brain from worsening as we age.
- **Balanced Nutrition:** This diet provides a balanced intake of essential nutrients, making it a sustainable choice for long-term health.

As you explore the recipes in this cookbook, you'll discover how the Mediterranean diet can promote your well-being and enhance your culinary experiences as a couple. Let's embark on this delicious journey together and savor the flavors of the Mediterranean.

Portion Control, Meal Planning, and Ingredient Substitutions for Smaller Servings

One of the key aspects of successfully adopting the Mediterranean diet for two is mastering portion control, efficient meal planning, and smart ingredient substitutions. By doing so, you can savor the flavors of the Mediterranean while maintaining a healthy balance. Here are some valuable tips to guide you:

1. Portion Control:

- **Invest in Smaller Serveware:** Use smaller plates, bowls, and utensils to control portion sizes naturally. This optical illusion can help prevent overeating.
- **Mindful Eating:** Take the time to savor each chomp. Put your fork between bites and engage in conversation to slow your eating pace.
- **Follow Recipe Servings:** Stick to the recommended servings in recipes. If a recipe serves four, consider halving it to create a perfect meal for two.
- **Pack Leftovers Right Away:** If you prepare a larger batch, immediately portion and store leftovers in the fridge or freezer to avoid temptation.

2. Meal Planning:

- **Weekly Menu:** Plan your meals for the week ahead. This diet reduces food waste, saves time, and helps you stay on track with your Mediterranean diet goals.
- **Balance Proteins:** Alternate between seafood, poultry, and vegetarian meals to ensure variety and balanced nutrition.
- **Incorporate Seasonal Produce:** Plan your meals around seasonal fruits and vegetables. They're fresher, more affordable, and packed with flavor.
- **Batch Cooking:** Prepare larger batches of staple items like grains, legumes, and sauces and use them in different weekly recipes.

3. Ingredient Substitutions for Smaller Servings:

- **Herbs and Spices:** Use herbs and spices liberally to enhance flavor without increasing portion sizes. Fresh herbs like basil and mint add freshness to dishes.
- **Half the Recipe:** When making recipes, especially those designed for larger families, halve the ingredients to match your needs.
- **Adjust Baking Recipes:** Baking recipes can be a bit trickier to adjust. For baked goods like muffins or cookies, consider freezing portions of the dough for future use.
- **Replace Heavy Cream:** In recipes that call for heavy cream, substitute with Greek yogurt and milk for a lighter yet creamy texture.

- **Choose Leaner Cuts:** When using red meat, opt for lean cuts like sirloin or tenderloin, which are healthier and cook faster.
- **Whole Grains:** Choose whole grains like quinoa, farro, or bulgur for added fiber and nutrients in smaller servings.

By incorporating these tips into your Mediterranean diet journey, you'll find it easier to manage portion sizes, plan meals efficiently, and make ingredient substitutions that suit your needs as a couple. This way, you can enjoy Mediterranean cuisine's delicious and healthful benefits without any unnecessary waste or excess.

Chapter 1:
Breakfast For Two

GREEK YOGURT PARFAIT

Servings: 2
Prep Time: 5 minutes

Nutrition Info (per serving):

- Calories: 250
- Protein: 15g
- Carbohydrates: 35g
- Dietary Fiber: 5g
- Sugars: 20g
- Fat: 6g
- Saturated Fat: 1g
- Cholesterol: 5mg
- Sodium: 60mg
- Potassium: 350mg

Ingredients:

- 1 cup Greek yogurt
- 1/2 cup granola (choose a low-sugar option)
- 1 cup mixed berries (strawberries, blueberries, raspberries)
- 2 tablespoons honey
- 1/4 cup chopped nuts (e.g., almonds, walnuts)

Directions:

1. Start with a layer of Greek yogurt in two serving glasses or bowls.
2. Put some granola on top of the yogurt.
3. Add a layer of mixed berries.
4. Drizzle a tablespoon of honey over each parfait.
5. Finish by sprinkling chopped nuts on top.
6. Serve immediately and enjoy your nutritious Greek yogurt parfait.

MEDITERRANEAN VEGETABLE OMELETTE

Servings: 2
Prep Time: 10 minutes

Nutrition Info (per serving):

- Calories: 250
- Protein: 14g
- Carbohydrates: 10g
- Dietary Fiber: 2g
- Sugars: 4g
- Fat: 18g
- Saturated Fat: 6g
- Cholesterol: 215mg
- Sodium: 450mg
- Potassium: 350mg

Ingredients:

- 4 large eggs
- 2 tablespoons olive oil
- Half a cup of bell peppers that have been cut into small pieces, including different colors of peppers.
- 1/2 cup diced tomatoes
- 1/4 cup diced red onion
- 1/4 cup crumbled feta cheese
- Salt and pepper to taste
- Fresh basil leaves for garnish

Directions:

1. Mix the eggs in a big bowl and add salt and pepper to make them taste good.
2. Warm up olive oil in a non-stick pan on medium heat.
3. Add diced bell peppers, tomatoes, and red onion to the skillet. Sauté for about 3-4 minutes until vegetables are tender.
4. Pour the whisked eggs into the skillet, covering the vegetables evenly.
5. Cook for 2-3 minutes until the edges set.
6. Sprinkle crumbled feta cheese over half of the omelet and fold the other half over the top.
7. Cook for another 1-2 minutes until the cheese melts and the omelet is fully set.
8. Garnish with fresh basil leaves and serve.

AVOCADO TOAST WITH POACHED EGGS

Servings: 2
Prep Time: 15 minutes

Nutrition Info (per serving):

- Calories: 320
- Protein: 12g
- Carbohydrates: 22g
- Dietary Fiber: 8g
- Sugars: 2g
- Fat: 22g
- Saturated Fat: 4g
- Cholesterol: 185mg
- Sodium: 250mg
- Potassium: 630mg

Ingredients:

- 2 slices whole-grain bread, toasted
- 1 ripe avocado, mashed
- 4 large eggs
- 1 tablespoon white vinegar
- Salt and pepper to taste
- Red pepper flakes (optional)
- Fresh parsley for garnish

Directions:

1. Toast the whole-grain bread slices until they're crispy.
2. While the bread is toasting, poach the eggs. Heat a pot of water to a gentle simmer and add the white vinegar. Be gentle when you break each egg into a little bowl and put them in warm water. Poach for about 3 minutes until the whites are set, but the yolks are still runny.
3. While the eggs poach, spread the mashed avocado evenly on the toasted bread slices.
4. Gently take out the poached eggs using a spoon with holes and put one on top of each piece of avocado toast.
5. Sprinkle some salt, pepper, or red pepper flakes on the food to add flavor to your food to add flavor.
6. Garnish with fresh parsley and serve immediately.

These Mediterranean diet breakfast recipes are designed to provide a balanced, flavorful, and nutritious start to your day for two people. Enjoy your Mediterranean-inspired breakfasts!

MEDITERRANEAN FRITTATA

Servings: 2
Prep Time: 15 minutes

Nutrition Info (per serving):

- Calories: 280
- Protein: 14g
- Carbohydrates: 15g
- Dietary Fiber: 3g
- Sugars: 5g
- Fat: 18g
- Saturated Fat: 6g
- Cholesterol: 215mg
- Sodium: 550mg
- Potassium: 400mg

Ingredients:

- 4 large eggs
- 1/2 cup cherry tomatoes, halved
- 1/4 cup sliced black olives

- 1/4 cup crumbled feta cheese
- 2 tablespoons chopped fresh basil
- Salt and pepper to taste
- 1 tablespoon olive oil

Directions:

1. Preheat your oven's broiler.
2. In a bowl, whisk the eggs and sprinkle salt and pepper.
3. Warm up olive oil in a skillet that can be used in the oven on medium heat.
4. Add cherry tomatoes and black olives to the skillet and sauté for 2-3 minutes.
5. Pour the whisked eggs evenly over the tomato and olive mixture.
6. Sprinkle crumbled feta cheese and chopped basil over the eggs.
7. Cook on the stovetop for 3-4 minutes until the edges are set.
8. Put the skillet in the oven and cook under the broiler for 2-3 minutes until the top turns golden and the frittata becomes firm.
9. Take out of the oven, cut into pieces, and give to someone to eat.

MEDITERRANEAN CHIA PUDDING

Servings: 2
Prep Time: 5 minutes (plus chilling time)

Nutrition Info (per serving):

- Calories: 200
- Protein: 6g
- Carbohydrates: 25g
- Dietary Fiber: 9g
- Sugars: 8g
- Fat: 9g
- Saturated Fat: 1g
- Cholesterol: 0mg
- Sodium: 100mg
- Potassium: 260mg

Ingredients:

- 1/4 cup chia seeds

- One glass of plain almond milk. (or any milk of your choice)
- 1/2 teaspoon pure vanilla extract
- 1 tablespoon honey or maple syrup
- 1/2 cup mixed berries (strawberries, blueberries, raspberries)
- 2 tablespoons chopped nuts (e.g., almonds, walnuts)

Directions:

1. Mix chia seeds, almond milk, vanilla extract, and honey in a bowl.
2. Put a cover on it in the refrigerator for 4 hours or overnight. Stir it now and then until it becomes thick like pudding.
3. Divide the chia pudding into two serving glasses or bowls.
4. Top each with mixed berries and chopped nuts.
5. Drizzle with additional honey or maple syrup if desired.
6. Serve chilled.

MEDITERRANEAN OATMEAL BOWL

Servings: 2
Prep Time: 10 minutes

Nutrition Info (per serving):

- Calories: 320
- Protein: 9g
- Carbohydrates: 46g
- Dietary Fiber: 6g
- Sugars: 14g
- Fat: 11g
- Saturated Fat: 2g
- Cholesterol: 5mg
- Sodium: 120mg
- Potassium: 400mg

Ingredients:
- 1 cup rolled oats
- two cups unsweetened almond milk (or any milk of your choice)
- 1/2 teaspoon ground cinnamon
- 1/4 cup chopped dried apricots
- 1/4 cup chopped nuts (e.g., pistachios, almonds)
- 2 tablespoons honey
- 1/2 cup sliced fresh figs (or other seasonal fruits)

Directions:
1. Combine rolled oats, almond milk, and ground cinnamon in a saucepan.
2. Heat the mixture slowly until it starts gently bubbling. Then, lower the heat and let it cook for 5-7 minutes. Stir from time to time. Keep cooking until the oats become smooth and reach the texture you like. Divide the oatmeal into two bowls.
3. Top with chopped dried apricots, nuts, and a drizzle of honey.
4. Garnish with sliced fresh figs or other seasonal fruits.
5. Serve warm, and enjoy your Mediterranean-inspired oatmeal bowl.

These additional Mediterranean diet breakfast recipes provide even more options for a healthy and delicious start to your day as a couple. Enjoy your breakfast!

MEDITERRANEAN SHAKSHUKA

Servings: 2
Prep Time: 15 minutes

Nutrition Info (per serving):

- Calories: 250
- Protein: 12g
- Carbohydrates: 12g
- Dietary Fiber: 4g
- Sugars: 6g
- Fat: 17g
- Saturated Fat: 4g
- Cholesterol: 215mg
- Sodium: 580mg
- Potassium: 620mg

Ingredients:

- 1 tablespoon olive oil
- 1/2 cup diced onion

- Half a cup of bell peppers of different colors have been chopped up.
- 2 cloves garlic, minced
- 1 teaspoon ground cumin
- 1 teaspoon paprika
- 1/2 teaspoon cayenne pepper (adjust to taste)
- 1 can (14 ounces) diced tomatoes
- 4 large eggs
- Salt and pepper to taste
- Fresh parsley or cilantro for garnish
- Feta cheese for topping (optional)

Directions:

1. Warm up olive oil in a pan on medium heat.
2. Add diced onions and bell peppers, and sauté until softened for about 4-5 minutes.
3. Stir in minced garlic, ground cumin, paprika, and cayenne pepper. Cook for 1-2 more minutes until it smells good.
4. Pour the diced tomatoes and simmer for 10-12 minutes until the sauce thickens.
5. Make four small wells in the tomato mixture and crack an egg into each well.
6. Cover the skillet and cook for 5-7 minutes until the egg whites are set but the yolks are still runny.
7. Add salt and pepper to your food, and decorate it with fresh parsley or cilantro. You can also add crumbled feta cheese on top if you like.
8. Serve hot with crusty whole-grain bread for dipping.

MEDITERRANEAN SMOOTHIE BOWL

Servings: 2
Prep Time: 10 minutes

Nutrition Info (per serving):

- Calories: 280
- Protein: 12g
- Carbohydrates: 45g
- Dietary Fiber: 8g
- Sugars: 20g
- Fat: 8g
- Saturated Fat: 1g
- Cholesterol: 5mg
- Sodium: 180mg
- Potassium: 600mg

Ingredients:

- 2 ripe bananas, frozen
- 1 cup unsweetened Greek yogurt
- 1/2 cup unsweetened almond milk (or any milk of your choice)
- one tablespoon honey
- 1/4 cup rolled oats
- 1/2 cup mixed berries (strawberries, blueberries, raspberries)
- 2 tablespoons chopped nuts (e.g., almonds, walnuts)
- Fresh mint leaves for garnish

Directions:

1. Combine frozen bananas, Greek yogurt, almond milk, honey, and rolled oats in a blender.
2. Blend until smooth and creamy.
3. Divide the smoothie mixture into two bowls.
4. Top each bowl with mixed berries, chopped nuts, and fresh mint leaves.
5. Drizzle with an additional touch of honey if desired.
6. Serve immediately with a spoon.

MEDITERRANEAN BREAKFAST BURRITO

Servings: 2
Prep Time: 20 minutes

Nutrition Info (per serving):

- Calories: 320
- Protein: 14g
- Carbohydrates: 26g
- Dietary Fiber: 6g
- Sugars: 4g
- Fat: 18g
- Saturated Fat: 5g
- Cholesterol: 190mg
- Sodium: 560mg
- Potassium: 470mg

Ingredients:

- 4 large eggs
- 2 whole-grain tortillas
- 1/2 cup diced tomatoes
- 1/4 cup diced red onion
- 1/4 cup chopped fresh spinach
- 1/4 cup crumbled feta cheese
- 2 tablespoons chopped fresh parsley
- Salt and pepper to taste
- Olive oil for cooking

Directions:

1. In a bowl, blend the eggs and sprinkle in a little salt and pepper.
2. Heat olive oil in a skillet over medium heat.
3. Add diced tomatoes and red onion to the skillet and sauté for 2-3 minutes until softened.
4. Put chopped spinach in a pan and cook it for 1-2 minutes until it shrinks.
5. Put the beaten eggs into the pan and cook until they finish.
6. Heat the tortillas in a different pan or microwave.
7. Put an equal amount of the mixed scrambled eggs onto each tortilla.
8. Sprinkle crumbled feta cheese and chopped fresh parsley over the eggs.
9. Roll up the tortillas to create burritos.
10. Serve warm, and enjoy your Mediterranean breakfast burritos.

MEDITERRANEAN QUINOA BREAKFAST BOWL

Servings: 2
Prep Time: 15 minutes

Nutrition Info (per serving):

- Calories: 320
- Protein: 10g
- Carbohydrates: 48g
- Dietary Fiber: 7g
- Sugars: 11g
- Fat: 10g
- Saturated Fat: 1g
- Cholesterol: 0mg
- Sodium: 110mg
- Potassium: 420mg

Ingredients:

- 1 cup cooked quinoa
- 1/2 cup Greek yogurt
- 1/2 cup diced fresh mango
- 1/4 cup pomegranate seeds
- 2 tablespoons chopped pistachios
- 1 tablespoon honey
- Fresh mint leaves for garnish

Directions:

1. In a bowl, divide the cooked quinoa between two servings.
2. Top each bowl with Greek yogurt.
3. Add diced fresh mango and pomegranate seeds.
4. Sprinkle chopped pistachios over the top.
5. Drizzle with honey.
6. Garnish with fresh mint leaves.
7. Serve immediately and enjoy your Mediterranean quinoa breakfast bowl.

MEDITERRANEAN BREAKFAST WRAP

Servings: 2
Prep Time: 10 minutes

Nutrition Info (per serving):

- Calories: 290
- Protein: 11g
- Carbohydrates: 38g
- Dietary Fiber: 6g
- Sugars: 6g
- Fat: 10g
- Saturated Fat: 2g
- Cholesterol: 190mg
- Sodium: 490mg
- Potassium: 390mg

Ingredients:

- 2 whole-grain wraps or tortillas
- 4 large eggs, scrambled
- 1/2 cup diced cucumber
- 1/2 cup diced tomatoes
- 1/4 cup crumbled feta cheese
- 2 tablespoons chopped fresh dill
- Salt and pepper to taste
- Tzatziki sauce for drizzling (optional)

Directions:

1. Warm the whole-grain wraps or tortillas.
2. Divide the scrambled eggs evenly between the two wraps.
3. Add diced cucumber and diced tomatoes.
4. Sprinkle crumbled feta cheese and chopped fresh dill.
5. Season with salt and pepper to taste.
6. Drizzle with tzatziki sauce if desired.
7. Roll up the wraps, tucking in the sides to secure the fillings.
8. Serve warm, and enjoy your Mediterranean breakfast wraps.

MEDITERRANEAN ACAI BOWL

Servings: 2
Prep Time: 10 minutes

Nutrition Info (per serving):

- Calories: 280
- Protein: 6g
- Carbohydrates: 42g
- Dietary Fiber: 8g
- Sugars: 27g
- Fat: 12g
- Saturated Fat: 2g
- Cholesterol: 0mg
- Sodium: 40mg
- Potassium: 430mg

Ingredients:

- 2 packets (4 ounces) of frozen acai puree
- The amount of unsweetened almond milk needed is 1/2 cup. You can also use any other type of milk that you prefer.
- 2 ripe bananas, frozen

- 1/2 cup mixed berries (strawberries, blueberries, raspberries)
- 1/4 cup granola
- 2 tablespoons shredded coconut
- Fresh berries for topping

Directions:

1. Combine the frozen acai puree, almond milk, and bananas in a blender.
2. Blend until smooth and creamy.
3. Divide the acai mixture into two serving bowls.
4. Top each bowl with mixed berries, granola, shredded coconut, and fresh berries.
5. Serve immediately with a spoon.

TOMATO TOASTS WITH MINT YOGURT AND SUMAC VINAIGRETTE

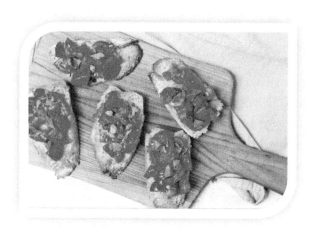

Servings: 2
Prep Time: 15 minutes

Nutrition Info (per serving):

- Calories: 280
- Protein: 10g
- Carbohydrates: 32g
- Dietary Fiber: 6g
- Sugars: 8g
- Fat: 14g
- Saturated Fat: 2g
- Cholesterol: 5mg
- Sodium: 350mg
- Potassium: 620mg

Ingredients:

- 2 slices whole-grain bread, toasted
- 1 cup cherry tomatoes, halved

- 1/2 cup Greek yogurt
- 1 tablespoon fresh mint leaves, chopped
- 1/2 teaspoon sumac spice
- 1 tablespoon olive oil
- Salt and pepper to taste

Directions:

1. Combine Greek yogurt, chopped fresh mint, and a pinch of salt in a bowl. Mix well.
2. Toss cherry tomato halves with olive oil, sumac spice, salt, and pepper in another bowl.
3. Spread the mint yogurt mixture on the toasted whole-grain bread slices.
4. Top with the seasoned cherry tomatoes.
5. Serve immediately, and enjoy your Tomato Toast with Mint Yogurt and Sumac Vinaigrette.

SPINACH AND GOAT CHEESE EGG MUFFINS

Servings: 2 (6 egg muffins total)
Prep Time: 20 minutes

Nutrition Info (per serving, 3 muffins):

- Calories: 320
- Protein: 18g
- Carbohydrates: 7g
- Dietary Fiber: 2g
- Sugars: 2g
- Fat: 24g
- Saturated Fat: 9g
- Cholesterol: 310mg
- Sodium: 480mg
- Potassium: 420mg

Ingredients:

- 6 large eggs
- 1 cup fresh spinach, chopped
- 1/4 cup crumbled goat cheese
- 1/4 cup diced red bell pepper
- 1/4 cup diced red onion
- Salt and pepper to taste
- Olive oil for greasing the muffin tin

Directions:

1. Turn on your oven and set it to 350 degrees Fahrenheit (175 degrees Celsius) before using it. Put some olive oil on a muffin tin to prevent sticking.
2. In a bowl, combine the eggs and sprinkle in some salt and pepper.
3. Distribute chopped spinach, diced red bell pepper, diced red onion, and crumbled goat cheese evenly among the muffin tin cups.
4. Pour the whisked eggs over the fillings in each cup.
5. Bake in the oven for about 15-18 minutes or until the egg muffins are set and slightly golden on top.
6. Let them cool a little bit before taking them out of the muffin tray.
7. Serve warm, and enjoy your Spinach and Goat Cheese Egg Muffins.

SNOW PEA AND RICOTTA TOASTS

Servings: 2
Prep Time: 10 minutes

Nutrition Info (per serving):

- Calories: 260
- Protein: 10g
- Carbohydrates: 28g
- Dietary Fiber: 4g
- Sugars: 3g
- Fat: 13g
- Saturated Fat: 4g
- Cholesterol: 15mg
- Sodium: 330mg
- Potassium: 320mg

Ingredients:

- 2 slices whole-grain bread, toasted
- 1 cup snow peas, thinly sliced
- 1/2 cup ricotta cheese

- Zest of 1 lemon
- 1 tablespoon fresh mint leaves, chopped
- Olive oil for drizzling
- Salt and pepper to taste

Directions:

1. Combine ricotta cheese, lemon zest, chopped fresh mint, salt, and pepper in a bowl. Mix well.
2. Spread the ricotta mixture on the toasted whole-grain bread slices.
3. Top with thinly sliced snow peas.
4. Drizzle with olive oil and add an extra sprinkle of chopped mint if desired.
5. Serve immediately, and enjoy your Snow peas and Ricotta toast.

SHEET PAN EGG TACOS

Servings: 2
Prep Time: 15 minutes

Nutrition Info (per serving):

- Calories: 320
- Protein: 15g
- Carbohydrates: 24g
- Dietary Fiber: 6g
- Sugars: 6g
- Fat: 18g
- Saturated Fat: 4g
- Cholesterol: 375mg
- Sodium: 480mg
- Potassium: 400mg

Ingredients:

- 4 small whole-wheat tortillas
- 4 large eggs

- 1 cup black beans, drained and rinsed
- 1 cup diced bell peppers (assorted colors)
- 1 cup diced red onion
- 1/2 cup diced tomatoes
- 1/2 cup shredded cheddar cheese
- Olive oil for drizzling
- Salt and pepper to taste
- Fresh cilantro for garnish

Directions:

1. Turn on your oven and set the temperature to 375 degrees Fahrenheit (or 190 degrees Celsius).
2. Place the whole-wheat tortillas on a baking sheet.
3. Toss diced bell peppers, red onion, and tomatoes. In a dish, mix olive oil, salt, and pepper.
4. Spread the vegetable mixture evenly on the tortillas.
5. Create a well in the center of each tortilla and carefully crack an egg into each well.
6. Sprinkle black beans and shredded cheddar cheese around the eggs.
7. Put it in the oven for around 12-15 minutes until the egg whites are solid but the yolks are still soft.
8. Garnish with fresh cilantro and serve your Sheet Pan Egg Tacos.

BLUEBERRY-AND-MIXED NUT PARFAIT

Servings: 2
Prep Time: 10 minutes

Nutrition Info (per serving):

- Calories: 290
- Protein: 8g
- Carbohydrates: 34g
- Dietary Fiber: 5g
- Sugars: 18g
- Fat: 15g
- Saturated Fat: 2g
- Cholesterol: 5mg
- Sodium: 40mg
- Potassium: 360mg

Ingredients:

- 1 cup Greek yogurt
- 1 cup fresh blueberries
- 1/2 cup mixed nuts (e.g., almonds, walnuts, cashews), chopped
- 2 tablespoons honey
- 1/4 cup granola

Directions:

1. Start with a layer of Greek yogurt in two serving glasses or bowls.
2. Add a layer of fresh blueberries.
3. Sprinkle a generous layer of mixed nuts over the blueberries.
4. Drizzle honey over each parfait.
5. Finish with a layer of granola for added crunch.
6. Serve immediately and enjoy your Blueberry-and-Mixed Nut Parfait.

SALMON HASH WITH SUNNY-SIDE-UP EGGS

Servings: 2
Prep Time: 20 minutes

Nutrition Info (per serving):

- Calories: 330
- Protein: 20g
- Carbohydrates: 18g
- Dietary Fiber: 4g
- Sugars: 2g
- Fat: 20g
- Saturated Fat: 5g
- Cholesterol: 220mg
- Sodium: 430mg
- Potassium: 570mg

Ingredients:

- 2 cups cooked salmon, flaked
- 2 cups diced potatoes
- 1/2 cup diced red bell pepper
- 1/2 cup diced red onion
- 2 cloves garlic, minced
- 2 large eggs
- 2 tablespoons olive oil
- Salt and pepper to taste
- Fresh dill for garnish

Directions:

1. Warm up some olive oil in a frying pan on medium heat.
2. Add diced potatoes and cook until they brown and become tender, about 7-8 minutes.
3. Stir in diced red bell pepper, red onion, and minced garlic. Keep cooking for 3-4 minutes until the vegetables become tender.
4. Add flaked salmon to the skillet and cook for 2-3 minutes to heat through.
5. Create two wells in the mixture and carefully crack a large egg into each well.
6. Cover the skillet and cook for 3-4 minutes until the egg whites are set but the yolks are still runny.
7. Sprinkle salt and pepper on top, add fresh dill for decoration, and serve your Salmon Hash with Sunny-Side Eggs.

CURRY-AVOCADO CRISPY EGG TOAST

Servings: 2
Prep Time: 15 minutes

Nutrition Info (per serving):

- Calories: 320
- Protein: 12g
- Carbohydrates: 28g
- Dietary Fiber: 6g
- Sugars: 4g
- Fat: 19g
- Saturated Fat: 3g
- Cholesterol: 190mg
- Sodium: 470mg
- Potassium: 450mg

Ingredients:

- 2 slices whole-grain bread, toasted
- 2 large eggs
- 1 ripe avocado, sliced
- 1 teaspoon curry powder
- Use a small amount, about 1/4 of a teaspoon, of red pepper flakes in your food. However, depending on how spicy you like it, you can add more or less.
- Salt and pepper to taste
- Fresh cilantro for garnish

Directions:

1. Mix sliced avocado with curry powder, red pepper flakes, salt, and pepper in a bowl.
2. Spread the seasoned avocado slices on the toasted whole-grain bread slices.
3. Heat some olive oil in a frying pan on medium heat.
4. Carefully crack a large egg into the skillet and cook until the whites are set and the yolks are still runny.
5. Place the crispy fried egg on top of the avocado on each toast.
6. Garnish with fresh cilantro.
7. Serve your Curry-Avocado Crispy Egg Toast while hot.

STRESS LESS SMOOTHIE

Servings: 2
Prep Time: 5 minutes

Nutrition Info (per serving):

- Calories: 280
- Protein: 12g
- Carbohydrates: 38g
- Dietary Fiber: 7g
- Sugars: 22g
- Fat: 10g
- Saturated Fat: 1g
- Cholesterol: 0mg
- Sodium: 90mg
- Potassium: 530mg

Ingredients:

- 2 ripe bananas
- For this recipe, you should have one cup of almond milk
- 1/2 cup rolled oats

- 1 tablespoon honey
- 1/2 teaspoon ground cinnamon
- 1/2 cup fresh spinach leaves
- A half cup of frozen berries includes strawberries, blueberries, and raspberries.

Directions:

1. Combine ripe bananas, almond milk, rolled oats, honey, and ground cinnamon in a blender.
2. Blend until smooth and creamy.
3. Add fresh spinach leaves and frozen mixed berries.
4. Mix again until all ingredients are well mixed together.
5. Divide the smoothie into two glasses.
6. Serve your Stress Less Smoothie chilled.

SPINACH-CURRY CREPES

Servings: 2
Prep Time: 20 minutes

Nutrition Info (per serving):

- Calories: 320
- Protein: 10g
- Carbohydrates: 26g
- Dietary Fiber: 4g
- Sugars: 2g
- Fat: 20g
- Saturated Fat: 4g
- Cholesterol: 85mg
- Sodium: 480mg
- Potassium: 310mg

Ingredients:

For the Crepes:

- 1 cup chickpea flour
- 1 cup water
- 1 tablespoon olive oil

- 1/2 teaspoon curry powder
- Salt and pepper to taste

For the Filling:

- 2 cups fresh spinach leaves
- 1/2 cup crumbled feta cheese
- 1/4 cup diced red onion
- 1/4 cup chopped fresh cilantro
- Olive oil for cooking

Directions: For the Crepes:

1. Whisk chickpea flour, water, olive oil, curry powder, salt, and pepper until you have a smooth batter.
2. Warm up a pan that doesn't stick to food on medium heat and add olive oil.
3. Pour a ladleful batter into the skillet, swirling it to coat the bottom evenly.
4. Cook for 2-3 minutes until the crepe sets and the edges start to lift.
5. Turn the crepe over and cook for 1-2 more minutes. Repeat with the remaining batter.
6. Keep the crepes warm while you prepare the filling.

For the Filling:

1. In the same skillet, add a bit of olive oil if needed.
2. Sauté diced red onion until translucent.
3. Put fresh spinach leaves in a pan and cook them until they become soft and shrivel.
4. Place a portion of the spinach mixture in the center of each crepe.
5. Sprinkle crumbled feta cheese and chopped fresh cilantro over the spinach.
6. Fold the crepes over the filling.
7. Serve your Spinach-Curry Crepes while hot.

Chapter 2:
Appetizers and Snacks

MEDITERRANEAN HUMMUS AND VEGGIE PLATTER

Servings: 2
Prep Time: 10 minutes
Cook Time: 0 minutes

Nutrition Info (per serving):

- Calories: 320
- Protein: 10g
- Carbohydrates: 28g
- Dietary Fiber: 10g
- Sugars: 6g
- Fat: 20g
- Saturated Fat: 3g
- Cholesterol: 0mg
- Sodium: 470mg
- Potassium: 680mg

Ingredients:

For the Hummus:

- 1 cup canned chickpeas, drained and rinsed

- 2 tablespoons tahini
- 2 tablespoons lemon juice
- 2 cloves garlic, minced
- 2 tablespoons olive oil
- Salt and pepper to taste
- Pinch of ground cumin (optional)
- Water (as needed for desired consistency)

For the Veggie Platter:

- 1 cup cherry tomatoes, halved
- 1 cup cucumber, sliced
- 1 cup bell pepper strips (assorted colors)
- 1 cup baby carrots
- 1/2 cup Kalamata olives
- 1/2 cup sliced cucumbers
- 1/2 cup radishes, sliced
- Fresh parsley leaves for garnish (optional)

Directions:

For the Hummus:

1. Mix the chickpeas drained and washed in a machine that blends food, tahini, lemon juice, minced garlic, olive oil, salt, pepper, and ground cumin (if you want to add it).
2. Blend it until the mixture becomes smooth and creamy. If it's too thick, add a little water, one tablespoon at a time, until you achieve your desired consistency.
3. Try the food and change the seasoning if you need to. Add more lemon juice, salt, or pepper if it tastes bad.
4. Put the hummus in a bowl and pour a little olive oil over it.

For the Veggie Platter:

1. Arrange the cherry tomatoes, cucumber slices, bell pepper strips, baby carrots, Kalamata olives, sliced cucumbers, and radishes on a large serving platter.
2. Place a bowl of freshly made hummus in the center of the platter.
3. Garnish the hummus and veggies with fresh parsley leaves for added color and freshness.
4. Serve the Mediterranean Hummus and Veggie Platter as a light and healthy appetizer or snack for two. Enjoy!

GREEK TZATZIKI DIP WITH PITA CHIPS

Servings: 2
Prep Time: 15 minutes
Chilling Time: 30 minutes (optional)

Nutrition Info (per serving, including pita chips):

- Calories: 280
- Protein: 8g
- Carbohydrates: 38g
- Dietary Fiber: 2g
- Sugars: 3g
- Fat: 11g
- Saturated Fat: 2g
- Cholesterol: 5mg
- Sodium: 550mg
- Potassium: 180mg

Ingredients:

For the Tzatziki Dip:

- 1/2 cup Greek yogurt (full-fat or low-fat)
- 1/2 cucumber, grated and drained
- 1 clove garlic, minced
- 1 tablespoon fresh dill, finely chopped
- 1 tablespoon fresh mint, finely chopped (optional)
- 1 tablespoon extra-virgin olive oil
- 1/2 tablespoon lemon juice
- Salt and pepper to taste

For the Pita Chips:

- 2 whole wheat pita bread rounds
- 1 tablespoon olive oil
- 1/2 teaspoon dried oregano (optional)
- Salt to taste

Directions:

For the Tzatziki Dip:

1. Start by grating the cucumber. Get a box grater and grate the cucumber into a strainer with small holes over a bowl. Press down on the grated cucumber to remove excess moisture. Allow it to drain for about 5 minutes.
2. Mix the Greek yogurt, minced garlic, chopped dill, chopped mint (if using), extra-virgin olive oil, and lemon juice in a bowl.
3. Add the grated and drained cucumber to the yogurt mixture. Stir to combine.
4. Season the tzatziki dip with salt and pepper to taste. Adjust the seasoning according to your preference.
5. If you have enough time, put the tzatziki dip in the fridge for about 30 minutes so that the flavors mix. This step is optional but enhances the taste.

For the Pita Chips:

1. Turn on your oven and set it to 375 degrees Fahrenheit (190 degrees Celsius).
2. Cut each whole wheat pita bread round into 8 triangles, similar to pizza slices.
3. Put the pita pieces on a baking sheet covered with parchment paper.
4. Drizzle the olive oil over the pita triangles and sprinkle them with dried oregano (if used) and a salt pinch.
5. Toss the pita triangles to ensure they are coated evenly with the oil and seasonings.
6. Put the pita triangles in one row on the baking sheet.

7. Bake in the oven for 9-10 minutes or until the pita chips are golden brown and crispy. Keep an eye on them to prevent burning.

To Serve:

1. Once the pita chips are ready and the tzatziki dip has chilled (if desired), serve them together.
2. Enjoy your homemade Greek Tzatziki Dip with Pita Chips as a refreshing and satisfying snack for two!

This classic Greek dip paired with crispy pita chips is a delightful, healthy, Mediterranean-inspired snack. Perfect for sharing or enjoying as an appetizer for two.

STUFFED GRAPE LEAVES (DOLMAS)

Servings: 2 (approximately 6 stuffed grape leaves each)
Prep Time: 30 minutes
Cook Time: 45 minutes

Nutrition Info (per serving, approximately 6 dolmas):

- Calories: 210
- Protein: 5g
- Carbohydrates: 36g
- Dietary Fiber: 3g
- Sugars: 3g
- Fat: 5g
- Saturated Fat: 1g
- Cholesterol: 0mg
- Sodium: 470mg
- Potassium: 400mg

Ingredients:

For the Filling:

- 1/2 cup long-grain white rice, rinsed and drained

- 1 cup water
- 1 small onion, finely chopped
- 2 tablespoons fresh dill, finely chopped
- 2 tablespoons fresh mint, finely chopped
- 1/4 cup pine nuts or chopped walnuts (optional)
- Salt and pepper to taste

For the Grape Leaves:

- 12-14 grape leaves (from a jar, preserved in brine or freshly blanched)
- 1 lemon, thinly sliced
- 2 tablespoons extra-virgin olive oil

For the Cooking Liquid:

- 1 cup water
- 1/2 lemon, juiced
- 2 tablespoons extra-virgin olive oil

Directions:

Preparing the Grape Leaves:

1. If you're using grape leaves preserved in brine, remove them from the jar, rinse them under cold water, and let them drain.
2. If you're using fresh grape leaves, blanch them in boiling water for about 1-2 minutes until they soften, then drain and rinse under cold water.

Preparing the Filling:

1. Combine the rinsed white rice in a medium saucepan and 1 cup of water. Place the pot at a high temperature until the liquid inside begins to bubble and boil. Lower the heat, cover the pot, and let it cook gently for around 10 minutes or until the rice is almost cooked and has soaked up most of the water. Remove from heat and let it cool.
2. In a mixing bowl, combine the partially cooked rice, finely chopped onion, fresh dill, fresh mint, and pine nuts (if using). Season with salt and pepper to taste. Mix well to create the filling.

Assembling the Dolmas:

1. Lay a grape leaf flat on a clean work surface, vein-side up. Trim the stem if it's too long.
2. Put approximately 1 tablespoon of the rice filling close to the part where the stem of the grape leaf begins.

3. Fold the sides of the leaf over the filling, then roll it tightly from the stem end to the tip, creating a small cylinder. Repeat this process for the remaining grape leaves and filling.

Cooking the Dolmas:

1. In a pot or saucepan, arrange a layer of lemon slices on the bottom.
2. Carefully place the stuffed grape leaves seam-side down in the pot, creating a snug layer.
3. Put 2 tablespoons of olive oil on top of the stuffed grape leaves.
4. Mix 1 cup of water, the juice from 1/2 lemon, and 2 tablespoons of olive oil in a separate bowl. Pour this mixture over the dolmas.
5. Place a heatproof plate upside down on top of the stuffed grape leaves to hold them in place while cooking.
6. Put a lid on the pot and let it cook gently on low heat for around 40-45 minutes, or until the grape leaves become soft and the rice is completely cooked. Check occasionally and add more water if needed to prevent sticking.

To Serve:

1. Once the dolmas are cooked, remove them from the heat and let them cool slightly.
2. Serve the Stuffed Grape Leaves warm or at room temperature, with some lemon wedges on the side if desired.

GREEK SALAD SKEWERS

Servings: 2 (4 skewers per serving)
Prep Time: 20 minutes

Nutrition Info (per serving, 4 skewers):

- Calories: 150
- Protein: 6g
- Carbohydrates: 10g
- Dietary Fiber: 2g
- Sugars: 5g
- Fat: 11g
- Saturated Fat: 3g
- Cholesterol: 10mg
- Sodium: 340mg
- Potassium: 320mg

Ingredients:

- 1 cup cherry tomatoes
- 1 cucumber, cut into chunks
- 1 cup Kalamata olives, pitted

- 1 cup feta cheese, cut into cubes
- 1/2 red onion, cut into chunks
- 1/4 cup fresh basil leaves
- 2 tablespoons extra-virgin olive oil
- 1 tablespoon red wine vinegar
- 1/2 teaspoon dried oregano
- Salt and black pepper to taste
- Eight sticks made of wood were placed in water for 20 minutes.

Directions:

1. Mix the olive oil, red wine vinegar, dried oregano, salt, and black pepper in a bowl to make the salad dressing. Put aside.
2. Assemble the Greek Salad Skewers: Start by threading a cherry tomato onto a wooden skewer, followed by a chunk of cucumber, a Kalamata olive, a cube of feta cheese, a chunk of red onion, and a fresh basil leaf.
3. Repeat this process until each skewer has a variety of ingredients and you have used up all the salad components.
4. Arrange the assembled Greek Salad Skewers on a serving platter.
5. Drizzle the prepared salad dressing over the skewers, ensuring each gets a good amount of dressing.
6. Serve the Greek Salad Skewers immediately, and enjoy this refreshing and flavorful Mediterranean appetizer for two!

MEDITERRANEAN STUFFED MUSHROOMS

Servings: 2 (4 stuffed mushrooms each)
Prep Time: 20 minutes
Cook Time: 20 minutes

Nutrition Info (per serving, 4 stuffed mushrooms):

- Calories: 150
- Protein: 6g
- Carbohydrates: 8g
- Dietary Fiber: 2g
- Sugars: 2g
- Fat: 11g
- Saturated Fat: 3g
- Cholesterol: 15mg
- Sodium: 280mg
- Potassium: 420mg

Ingredients:

- Eight big white mushrooms, washed and with the stems taken out.

- 1/2 cup chopped spinach (fresh or frozen, thawed and drained)
- 1/4 cup crumbled feta cheese
- Two tablespoons of chopped sun-dried tomatoes (drain the oil).
- 1 clove garlic, minced
- 1/4 teaspoon dried oregano
- 1/4 teaspoon dried basil
- Salt and black pepper to taste
- 2 tablespoons extra-virgin olive oil
- Fresh parsley leaves for garnish (optional)

Directions:

1. Turn on your oven and set the temperature to 375°F (190°C). Spread some cooking oil or put a sheet of parchment paper on the baking dish.
2. Combine the chopped spinach, crumbled feta cheese, sun-dried tomatoes, minced garlic, dried oregano, dried basil, salt, and black pepper in a mixing bowl. Mix well to create the stuffing mixture.
3. Take each cleaned mushroom cap and stuff it with a spoonful of the Mediterranean filling. Press the filling down gently to ensure it's packed.
4. Place the stuffed mushrooms in the prepared baking dish.
5. Drizzle the extra-virgin olive oil over the stuffed mushrooms.
6. Bake in the oven for about 20 minutes or until the mushrooms are tender and the filling is lightly browned.
7. Once cooked, remove the Mediterranean Stuffed Mushrooms from the oven.
8. Garnish with fresh parsley leaves if desired.
9. Serve the stuffed mushrooms warm, and enjoy this flavorful Mediterranean appetizer for two!

GREEK YOGURT AND HONEY DIP WITH FRESH FRUIT

Servings: 2
Prep Time: 10 minutes

Nutrition Info (per serving):

- Calories: 150
- Protein: 6g
- Carbohydrates: 32g
- Dietary Fiber: 3g
- Sugars: 26g
- Fat: 1g
- Saturated Fat: 0g
- Cholesterol: 3mg
- Sodium: 25mg
- Potassium: 270mg

Ingredients:

For the Dip:

- 1/2 cup Greek yogurt (plain or vanilla, low-fat or full-fat)
- 2 tablespoons honey (adjust to taste)
- 1/2 teaspoon vanilla extract

For the Fresh Fruit:

- 1 apple, sliced
- 1 banana, sliced
- 1 cup berries (e.g., strawberries, blueberries, raspberries)
- Sliced citrus fruits (e.g., oranges, grapefruits) (optional)

Directions:

1. Combine the Greek yogurt, honey, and vanilla extract in a small mixing bowl. Mix everything until all the ingredients are fully combined. Change the quantity of honey according to how sweet you want it to be.
2. Wash and prepare the fresh fruit by slicing the apple and banana and rinsing the berries. If using citrus fruits, remove the peel and slice them into segments.
3. Serve the Greek Yogurt and Honey Dip in a bowl or on a serving plate.
4. Arrange the sliced fruit around the dip bowl.
5. Use toothpicks, skewers, or fingers to dip the fresh fruit into the creamy yogurt and honey mixture.
6. Enjoy your Greek Yogurt and Honey Dip with Fresh Fruit as a healthy and satisfying snack for two!

MEDITERRANEAN ROASTED RED PEPPER AND WALNUT DIP (MUHAMMARA)

Servings: 2
Prep Time: 20 minutes

Nutrition Info (per serving):

- Calories: 180
- Protein: 4g
- Carbohydrates: 14g
- Dietary Fiber: 3g
- Sugars: 7g
- Fat: 13g
- Saturated Fat: 1g
- Cholesterol: 0mg
- Sodium: 220mg
- Potassium: 220mg

Ingredients:

<u>For the Dip:</u>

- Two big red bell peppers were cooked until soft, with the skin removed and the seeds removed.
- 1 cup walnuts, toasted
- 2 cloves garlic, minced
- 1/4 cup extra-virgin olive oil
- 2 tablespoons pomegranate molasses (or substitute with honey)
- 1 teaspoon ground cumin
- Use half a teaspoon of red pepper flakes, but adjust the amount according to your preference.
- Salt and pepper to taste

For Serving:

- Fresh vegetables (e.g., carrot sticks, cucumber slices, celery)
- Pita bread or pita chips

Directions:

<u>For the Dip:</u>

1. In a food processor, combine roasted red bell peppers, toasted walnuts, minced garlic, extra-virgin olive oil, pomegranate molasses (or honey), ground cumin, red pepper flakes, salt, and pepper.
2. Mix until the mixture becomes soft and well-mixed.
3. Taste and adjust the seasoning and spiciness level as desired.

To Serve:

1. Transfer the Muhammara dip to a serving bowl.
2. You can eat this with fresh veggies and pita bread or pita chips.

GREEK-INSPIRED STUFFED MINI PEPPERS

Servings: 2
Prep Time: 25 minutes

Nutrition Info (per serving):

- Calories: 150
- Protein: 4g
- Carbohydrates: 12g
- Dietary Fiber: 2g
- Sugars: 3g
- Fat: 10g
- Saturated Fat: 2g
- Cholesterol: 10mg
- Sodium: 220mg
- Potassium: 250mg

Ingredients:

For the Stuffed Peppers:

- 12 mini bell peppers, assorted colors

- 1 cup feta cheese, crumbled
- 1/4 cup of Kalamata olives, with the pits removed and cut into pieces.
- 2 tablespoons fresh oregano, chopped
- 2 tablespoons extra-virgin olive oil
- Salt and pepper to taste

For Garnish:

- Fresh oregano leaves

Directions:

1. Preheat your oven to 375°F (190°C).
2. Cut the tops off the mini bell peppers and remove the seeds.
3. Combine crumbled feta cheese, chopped Kalamata olives, fresh oregano, extra-virgin olive oil, salt, and pepper in a bowl.
4. Stuff each mini bell pepper with the feta cheese mixture.
5. Place the stuffed peppers on a baking sheet.
6. Bake in the oven for 15-18 minutes or until the peppers are tender and the filling is slightly golden.
7. Garnish with fresh oregano leaves before serving.

To Serve:

1. Arrange the Greek-Inspired Stuffed Mini Peppers on a platter.
2. Serve as a delicious Mediterranean-inspired appetizer or snack.

MEDITERRANEAN QUINOA SALAD CUPS

Servings: 2
Prep Time: 25 minutes

Nutrition Info (per serving):

- Calories: 220
- Protein: 7g
- Carbohydrates: 30g
- Dietary Fiber: 4g
- Sugars: 3g
- Fat: 9g
- Saturated Fat: 1g
- Cholesterol: 0mg
- Sodium: 220mg
- Potassium: 310mg

Ingredients:

For the Quinoa Salad:

- 1 cup quinoa, cooked and cooled
- 1/2 cup cucumber, diced
- 1/2 cup cherry tomatoes, halved

69

- 1/4 cup red onion, finely chopped
- 1/4 cup Kalamata olives, pitted and chopped
- 2 tablespoons fresh parsley, chopped
- 2 tablespoons feta cheese, crumbled
- 2 tablespoons extra-virgin olive oil
- 2 tablespoons lemon juice
- Salt and pepper to taste

For the Salad Cups:

- 8 large lettuce leaves (e.g., Romaine or butter lettuce)

Directions:

For the Quinoa Salad:

1. Mix cooked and cooled quinoa in a big bowl, cut cucumber, small tomatoes, finely chopped red onion, Kalamata olives, fresh parsley, broken feta cheese, high-quality olive oil, lemon juice, salt, and pepper.
2. Toss until all ingredients are well combined.
3. Taste and adjust seasoning as needed.

For the Salad Cups:

1. Wash and dry the lettuce leaves.
2. Spoon the Mediterranean quinoa salad into each lettuce leaf.
3. Serve the Mediterranean Quinoa Salad Cups as a fresh and satisfying Mediterranean-inspired appetizer or snack.

Chapter 3:
Salads and Soups

GREEK SALAD

Servings: 2
Prep Time: 15 minutes

Nutrition Info (per serving):

- Calories: 190
- Protein: 4g
- Carbohydrates: 13g
- Dietary Fiber: 3g
- Sugars: 6g
- Fat: 15g
- Saturated Fat: 3g
- Cholesterol: 10mg
- Sodium: 280mg
- Potassium: 430mg

Ingredients:

For the Salad:

- 4 cups Romaine lettuce, chopped
- 1 cup cucumber, diced
- 1 cup cherry tomatoes, halved
- 1/2 cup red onion, thinly sliced
- 1/2 cup Kalamata olives, pitted
- 1/2 cup feta cheese, crumbled

For the Greek Dressing:

- 3 tablespoons extra-virgin olive oil
- 2 tablespoons red wine vinegar
- 1 teaspoon dried oregano
- Salt and pepper to taste

Directions:

For the Greek Dressing:

1. Combine olive oil, red wine vinegar, dried oregano, salt, and pepper in a little bowl and stir them together. Put away or go somewhere else.

For the Salad:

2. Combine chopped Romaine lettuce, diced cucumber, halved cherry tomatoes, thinly sliced red onion, Kalamata olives, and crumbled feta cheese in a big bowl.
3. Drizzle the Greek dressing over the salad.
4. Toss to coat the ingredients evenly.
5. Serve the Greek Salad as a refreshing Mediterranean-inspired salad.

MEDITERRANEAN CHICKPEA SALAD

Servings: 2
Prep Time: 20 minutes

Nutrition Info (per serving):

- Calories: 220
- Protein: 7g
- Carbohydrates: 29g
- Dietary Fiber: 6g
- Sugars: 7g
- Fat: 9g
- Saturated Fat: 1g
- Cholesterol: 0mg
- Sodium: 260mg
- Potassium: 380mg

Ingredients:

For the Salad:

- 2 cups cooked chickpeas (canned or cooked from dry)
- 1 cup cucumber, diced
- 1 cup cherry tomatoes, halved

- 1/2 cup red bell pepper, diced
- 1/4 cup red onion, finely chopped
- 1/4 cup fresh parsley, chopped
- 1/4 cup feta cheese, crumbled

For the Lemon-Herb Dressing:

- 3 tablespoons extra-virgin olive oil
- Juice of 1 lemon
- 1 clove garlic, minced
- 1 teaspoon dried oregano
- Salt and pepper to taste

Directions:

For the Lemon-Herb Dressing:

1. Whisk together extra-virgin olive oil, lemon juice, minced garlic, dried oregano, salt, and pepper in a small bowl. Set aside.

For the Salad:

1. Combine cooked chickpeas, diced cucumber, halved cherry tomatoes, red bell pepper, finely chopped red onion, fresh parsley, and crumbled feta cheese in a large salad bowl.
2. Drizzle the Lemon-Herb Dressing over the salad.
3. Toss to coat the ingredients evenly.
4. Serve the Mediterranean Chickpea Salad as a nutritious and satisfying salad.

MEDITERRANEAN TOMATO AND LENTIL SOUP

Servings: 2
Prep Time: 15 minutes
Cook Time: 30 minutes

Nutrition Info (per serving):

- Calories: 220
- Protein: 10g
- Carbohydrates: 30g
- Dietary Fiber: 10g
- Sugars: 6g
- Fat: 7g
- Saturated Fat: 1g
- Cholesterol: 0mg
- Sodium: 680mg
- Potassium: 720mg

Ingredients:

For the Soup:

- 1 cup dried brown or green lentils, rinsed and drained
- 1 onion, finely chopped
- 2 cloves garlic, minced
- 1 carrot, diced
- 1 celery stalk, diced
- 1 can (14 ounces) diced tomatoes
- 4 cups vegetable broth
- 2 teaspoons dried oregano
- 1 teaspoon ground cumin
- Salt and pepper to taste
- 2 tablespoons extra-virgin olive oil
- Fresh parsley for garnish

Directions:

1. In a large pot, heat the extra-virgin olive oil over medium heat.
2. Add the chopped onion, minced garlic, carrot, and celery. Sauté for about 5 minutes or until the vegetables are softened.
3. Add the rinsed lentils, diced tomatoes (with their juice), dried oregano, ground cumin, salt, and pepper. Stir to combine.
4. Add the vegetable broth and heat the soup until it begins to bubble.
5. Reduce the heat, cover, and simmer for about 25-30 minutes or until the lentils are tender.
6. Taste and adjust the seasoning as needed.
7. Serve the Mediterranean Tomato and Lentil Soup garnished with fresh parsley.

MEDITERRANEAN QUINOA SALAD

Servings: 2
Prep Time: 20 minutes

Nutrition Info (per serving):

- Calories: 250
- Protein: 8g
- Carbohydrates: 33g
- Dietary Fiber: 6g
- Sugars: 5g
- Fat: 10g
- Saturated Fat: 1g
- Cholesterol: 0mg
- Sodium: 330mg
- Potassium: 470mg

Ingredients:

For the Salad:

- 1 cup quinoa, cooked and cooled

- 1 cup cucumber, diced
- 1 cup cherry tomatoes, halved
- 1/2 cup red bell pepper, diced
- 1/4 cup red onion, finely chopped
- 1/4 cup of Kalamata olives that have had their pits removed and have been cut into small pieces.
- 1/4 cup fresh parsley, chopped
- 1/4 cup crumbled feta cheese

For the Lemon-Olive Oil Dressing:

- 3 tablespoons extra-virgin olive oil
- Juice of 1 lemon
- 1 clove garlic, minced
- 1/2 teaspoon dried oregano
- Salt and pepper to taste

Directions:

For the Lemon-Olive Oil Dressing:

1. Whisk together extra-virgin olive oil, lemon juice, minced garlic, dried oregano, salt, and pepper in a small bowl. Set aside.

For the Salad:

2. Combine cooked quinoa, diced cucumber, halved cherry tomatoes, red bell pepper, finely chopped red onion, Kalamata olives, fresh parsley, and crumbled feta cheese in a large salad bowl.
3. Drizzle the Lemon-Olive Oil Dressing over the salad.
4. Toss to coat the ingredients evenly.
5. Serve the Mediterranean Quinoa Salad as a nutritious and flavorful salad.

MEDITERRANEAN LENTIL SOUP

Servings: 2
Prep Time: 15 minutes
Cook Time: 30 minutes

Nutrition Info (per serving):

- Calories: 220
- Protein: 10g
- Carbohydrates: 30g
- Dietary Fiber: 10g
- Sugars: 6g
- Fat: 7g
- Saturated Fat: 1g
- Cholesterol: 0mg
- Sodium: 680mg
- Potassium: 720mg

Ingredients:

For the Soup:

- 1 cup dried green or brown lentils, rinsed and drained
- 1 onion, finely chopped

- 2 cloves garlic, minced
- 2 carrots, diced
- 2 celery stalks, diced
- 1 can (14 ounces) diced tomatoes
- 4 cups vegetable broth
- 2 teaspoons dried thyme
- 1 teaspoon ground cumin
- Salt and pepper to taste
- 2 tablespoons extra-virgin olive oil
- Fresh parsley for garnish

Directions:

1. In a large pot, heat the extra-virgin olive oil over medium heat.
2. Add the chopped onion, minced garlic, carrots, and celery. Sauté for about 5 minutes or until the vegetables are softened.
3. Add the rinsed lentils, diced tomatoes (with their juice), dried thyme, ground cumin, salt, and pepper. Stir to combine.
4. Add the vegetable broth to the soup and heat it until it starts boiling.
5. Reduce the heat, cover, and simmer for about 25-30 minutes or until the lentils are tender.
6. Taste and adjust the seasoning as needed.
7. Serve the Mediterranean Lentil Soup garnished with fresh parsley.

MEDITERRANEAN TABBOULEH SALAD

Servings: 2
Prep Time: 20 minutes

Nutrition Info (per serving):

- Calories: 220
- Protein: 5g
- Carbohydrates: 31g
- Dietary Fiber: 6g
- Sugars: 3g
- Fat: 9g
- Saturated Fat: 1g
- Cholesterol: 0mg
- Sodium: 300mg
- Potassium: 400mg

Ingredients:

For the Salad:

- 1 cup bulgur wheat, cooked and cooled
- 1 cup cucumber, diced

- 1 cup cherry tomatoes, quartered
- 1/2 cup fresh parsley, chopped
- 1/4 cup fresh mint leaves, chopped
- 1/4 cup red onion, finely chopped

For the Lemon-Olive Oil Dressing:

- 3 tablespoons extra-virgin olive oil
- Juice of 2 lemons
- 1 clove garlic, minced
- Salt and pepper to taste

Directions:

For the Lemon-Olive Oil Dressing:

1. Mix olive oil, lemon juice, minced garlic, salt, and pepper in a small bowl. Put aside

For the Salad:

2. Combine cooked and cooled bulgur wheat, diced cucumber, quartered cherry tomatoes, chopped fresh parsley, chopped fresh mint leaves, and finely chopped red onion in a large salad bowl.
3. Drizzle the Lemon-Olive Oil Dressing over the salad.
4. Toss to coat the ingredients evenly.
5. Serve the Mediterranean Tabbouleh Salad as a refreshing and nutritious salad.

These Mediterranean diet-inspired salad and soup recipes offer a delightful way to savor Mediterranean cuisine's flavors and health benefits. Enjoy these tasty options!

KALE, QUINOA & APPLE SALAD

Servings: 2
Prep Time: 20 minutes

Nutrition Info (per serving):

- Calories: 280
- Protein: 7g
- Carbohydrates: 40g
- Dietary Fiber: 6g
- Sugars: 11g
- Fat: 11g
- Saturated Fat: 1g
- Cholesterol: 0mg
- Sodium: 280mg
- Potassium: 480mg

Ingredients:

For the Salad:

- 4 cups kale leaves, stemmed and chopped
- 1 cup cooked quinoa, cooled
- 1 apple, thinly sliced
- 1/2 cup pecans, toasted and chopped
- 1/4 cup dried cranberries
- 1/4 cup crumbled feta cheese (optional)

For the Lemon-Honey Dressing:

- 3 tablespoons extra-virgin olive oil
- Juice of 1 lemon
- 1 tablespoon honey
- Salt and pepper to taste

Directions:

For the Lemon-Honey Dressing:

1. Whisk together extra-virgin olive oil, lemon juice, honey, salt, and pepper in a small bowl. Set aside.

For the Salad:

2. In a big salad bowl, combine chopped kale, cooked and cooled quinoa, thinly sliced apple, toasted pecans, dried cranberries, and crumbled feta cheese (if using).
3. Drizzle the Lemon-Honey Dressing over the salad.
4. Toss to coat the ingredients evenly.
5. Serve the Kale, Quinoa, and apple Salad as a wholesome and satisfying salad.

CHOPPED SALAD WITH SALMON & CREAMY GARLIC DRESSING

Servings: 2
Prep Time: 25 minutes

Nutrition Info (per serving):

- Calories: 320
- Protein: 24g
- Carbohydrates: 20g
- Dietary Fiber: 4g
- Sugars: 6g
- Fat: 17g
- Saturated Fat: 3g
- Cholesterol: 60mg
- Sodium: 420mg
- Potassium: 580mg

Ingredients:

<u>For the Salad:</u>

- 8 cups mixed salad greens (e.g., Romaine, arugula, spinach)
- 2 cups cherry tomatoes, halved
- 1 cucumber, diced
- 1 red bell pepper, diced
- 1/4 cup red onion, finely chopped
- 1/4 cup Kalamata olives, pitted and chopped
- 2 (6-ounce) grilled salmon fillets, flaked

<u>For the Creamy Garlic Dressing:</u>

- 1/4 cup plain Greek yogurt
- 1 clove garlic, minced
- Juice of 1 lemon
- 2 tablespoons extra-virgin olive oil
- Salt and pepper to taste

Directions:

<u>For the Creamy Garlic Dressing:</u>

1. Whisk together plain Greek yogurt, minced garlic, lemon juice, extra-virgin olive oil, salt, and pepper in a small bowl. Set aside.

<u>For the Salad:</u>

1. Combine mixed salad greens, cherry tomatoes, diced cucumber, red bell pepper, finely chopped red onion, and chopped Kalamata olives in a large bowl.
2. Top the salad with the flaked grilled salmon.
3. Drizzle the Creamy Garlic Dressing over the salad.
4. Toss to coat the ingredients evenly.
5. Serve the Chopped Salad with Salmon and creamy Garlic Dressing as a nutritious and satisfying meal.

AVOCADO TUNA SALAD

Servings: 2
Prep Time: 15 minutes

Nutrition Info (per serving):

- Calories: 280
- Protein: 20g
- Carbohydrates: 10g
- Dietary Fiber: 5g
- Sugars: 2g
- Fat: 20g
- Saturated Fat: 3g
- Cholesterol: 30mg
- Sodium: 330mg
- Potassium: 630mg

Ingredients:

<u>For the Salad:</u>

- Two cans of tuna in water, weighing five ounces, with the liquid removed.
- 2 ripe avocados, diced
- 1/4 cup red onion, finely chopped
- 1/4 cup cherry tomatoes, halved
- 1/4 cup cucumber, diced
- 1/4 cup of Kalamata olives that have had the pits removed and been cut into small pieces.
- 2 tablespoons fresh parsley, chopped

<u>For the Lemon-Dijon Dressing:</u>

- 3 tablespoons extra-virgin olive oil
- Juice of 1 lemon
- 1 teaspoon Dijon mustard
- Salt and pepper to taste

Directions:

<u>For the Lemon-Dijon Dressing:</u>

1. Whisk together extra-virgin olive oil, lemon juice, Dijon mustard, salt, and pepper in a small bowl. Set aside.

<u>For the Salad:</u>

1. Combine drained tuna, diced avocados, finely chopped red onion, cherry tomatoes, cucumber, chopped Kalamata olives, and fresh parsley in a large salad bowl.
2. Drizzle the Lemon-Dijon Dressing over the salad.
3. Gently toss to coat the ingredients evenly.
4. Serve the Avocado Tuna Salad as a delicious and healthy salad.

LEMONY LENTIL SALAD WITH FETA

Servings: 2
Prep Time: 20 minutes

Nutrition Info (per serving):

- Calories: 280
- Protein: 12g
- Carbohydrates: 35g
- Dietary Fiber: 14g
- Sugars: 3g
- Fat: 11g
- Saturated Fat: 3g
- Cholesterol: 15mg
- Sodium: 430mg
- Potassium: 650mg

Ingredients:

For the Salad:

- One cup of brown or green lentils is already cooked and at room temperature.
- 1 cucumber, diced
- 1 red bell pepper, diced
- 1/2 cup red onion, finely chopped
- 1/4 cup fresh parsley, chopped
- 1/4 cup crumbled feta cheese

For the Lemon-Olive Oil Dressing:

- 3 tablespoons extra-virgin olive oil
- Juice of 2 lemons
- Zest of 1 lemon
- 1 clove garlic, minced
- Salt and pepper to taste

Directions:

For the Lemon-Olive Oil Dressing:

1. Mix olive oil, lemon juice, lemon zest, garlic, salt, and pepper in a small bowl. Put away or ignore for now.

For the Salad:

1. Combine cooked and cooled lentils, diced cucumber, red bell pepper, finely chopped red onion, fresh parsley, and crumbled feta cheese in a large salad bowl.
2. Drizzle the Lemon-Olive Oil Dressing over the salad.
3. Toss to coat the ingredients evenly.
4. Serve the Lemony Lentil Salad with Feta as a zesty and nutritious salad.

SALAD PRIMAVERA WITH CREAMY MUSTARD VINAIGRETTE

Servings: 2
Prep Time: 20 minutes

Nutrition Info (per serving):

- Calories: 220
- Protein: 6g
- Carbohydrates: 20g
- Dietary Fiber: 4g
- Sugars: 5g
- Fat: 14g
- Saturated Fat: 2g
- Cholesterol: 0mg
- Sodium: 240mg
- Potassium: 370mg

Ingredients:

<u>For the Salad:</u>

- 8 cups mixed salad greens (e.g., arugula, spinach, Romaine)
- 1 cup cherry tomatoes, halved
- 1 cup sliced bell peppers (assorted colors)
- 1 cup blanched green beans, cut into bite-sized pieces
- 1/4 cup red onion, thinly sliced
- 1/4 cup black olives, pitted and sliced
- 1/4 cup crumbled goat cheese

<u>For the Creamy Mustard Vinaigrette:</u>

- 3 tablespoons extra-virgin olive oil
- 2 tablespoons white wine vinegar
- 1 tablespoon Dijon mustard
- 1 clove garlic, minced
- 1 tablespoon Greek yogurt
- Salt and pepper to taste

Directions:

<u>For the Creamy Mustard Vinaigrette:</u>

1. Mix olive oil, vinegar, mustard, garlic, Greek yogurt, salt, and pepper in a small bowl. Put on hold or keep separate.

<u>For the Salad:</u>

2. Combine mixed salad greens, cherry tomatoes, sliced bell peppers, blanched green beans, thinly sliced red onion, black olives, and crumbled goat cheese in a large bowl.
3. Drizzle the Creamy Mustard Vinaigrette over the salad.
4. Toss to coat the ingredients evenly.
5. Serve the Salad Primavera with Creamy Mustard Vinaigrette as a colorful and delightful salad.

FALAFEL SALAD WITH LEMON-TAHINI DRESSING

Servings: 2
Prep Time: 25 minutes

Nutrition Info (per serving):

- Calories: 320
- Protein: 12g
- Carbohydrates: 28g
- Dietary Fiber: 6g
- Sugars: 4g
- Fat: 20g
- Saturated Fat: 3g
- Cholesterol: 0mg
- Sodium: 470mg
- Potassium: 380mg

Ingredients:

For the Salad:

- 8 falafel patties (store-bought or homemade)
- 8 cups mixed salad greens (e.g., Romaine, spinach, kale)
- 1 cucumber, diced
- 1 cup cherry tomatoes, halved
- 1/4 cup red onion, thinly sliced
- 1/4 cup Kalamata olives, pitted and sliced
- 1/4 cup crumbled feta cheese (optional)

For the Lemon-Tahini Dressing:

- 3 tablespoons tahini
- Juice of 2 lemons
- 1 clove garlic, minced
- 1/4 cup water
- Salt and pepper to taste

Directions:

For the Lemon-Tahini Dressing:

1. Whisk together tahini, lemon juice, minced garlic, water, salt, and pepper in a small bowl until smooth. Adjust the consistency with more water if needed. Set aside.

For the Salad:

1. Cook the falafel patties according to package instructions or make homemade falafel.
2. In a large salad bowl, combine mixed salad greens, diced cucumber, halved cherry tomatoes, thinly sliced red onion, Kalamata olives, and crumbled feta cheese (if using).
3. Place the cooked falafel patties on top of the salad.
4. Drizzle the Lemon-Tahini Dressing over the salad and falafel.
5. Serve the Falafel Salad with Lemon-Tahini Dressing as a satisfying and flavorful salad.

SLOW-COOKER CHICKEN AND CHICKPEA SOUP

Servings: 2
Prep Time: 15 minutes
Cook Time: 4 hours (on low setting)

Nutrition Info (per serving):

- Calories: 280
- Protein: 24g
- Carbohydrates: 26g
- Dietary Fiber: 7g
- Sugars: 6g
- Fat: 9g
- Saturated Fat: 2g
- Cholesterol: 60mg
- Sodium: 780mg
- Potassium: 560mg

Ingredients:

- 1 pound boneless, skinless chicken breasts or thighs
- 1 cup dried chickpeas, soaked overnight and drained (or use canned)
- 4 cups low-sodium chicken broth
- 1 onion, chopped
- 2 carrots, sliced
- 2 celery stalks, sliced
- 3 cloves garlic, minced
- 1 teaspoon dried thyme
- 1 teaspoon dried oregano
- Salt and pepper to taste
- 2 cups spinach leaves
- Juice of 1 lemon
- Fresh parsley for garnish

Directions:

1. Place the chicken breasts (or thighs), soaked chickpeas, chopped onion, sliced carrots, celery, minced garlic, dried thyme, dried oregano, salt, and pepper in a slow cooker.
2. Pour in the chicken broth and stir to combine.
3. Cover and cook on the low setting for 4 hours until the chicken is tender and the chickpeas are cooked.
4. Take out the cooked chicken from the slow cooker and tear it apart using two forks.
5. Return the shredded chicken to the slow cooker.
6. Mix the spinach leaves and lemon juice.
7. Taste and adjust the seasoning if needed.
8. Serve the Slow-Cooker Chicken and chickpea Soup garnished with fresh parsley.

VEGAN CABBAGE SOUP

Servings: 2
Prep Time: 15 minutes
Cook Time: 30 minutes

Nutrition Info (per serving):

- Calories: 140
- Protein: 3g
- Carbohydrates: 29g
- Dietary Fiber: 8g
- Sugars: 11g
- Fat: 2g
- Saturated Fat: 0g
- Cholesterol: 0mg
- Sodium: 550mg
- Potassium: 570mg

Ingredients:

- 1 small head of cabbage, shredded
- 1 onion, chopped
- 2 carrots, sliced
- 2 celery stalks, sliced
- 4 cups low-sodium vegetable broth
- 1 can (14 ounces) diced tomatoes
- 2 cloves garlic, minced
- 1 teaspoon dried thyme
- 1 teaspoon dried rosemary
- Salt and pepper to taste
- Juice of 1 lemon
- Fresh parsley for garnish

Directions:

1. In a large pot, heat a bit of water or vegetable broth over medium heat.
2. Add the chopped onion and minced garlic. Sauté until the onion is translucent.
3. Stir in the shredded cabbage, sliced carrots, and sliced celery. Cook for about 5 minutes, stirring occasionally.
4. Pour in the low-sodium vegetable broth and diced tomatoes (with their juice).
5. Add the dried thyme, dried rosemary, salt, and pepper.
6. Heat the soup until it starts bubbling, then lower the heat, cover it, and let it cook gently for around 20-25 minutes or until the vegetables are soft.
7. Stir in the lemon juice.
8. Taste and adjust the seasoning if needed.
9. Serve the Vegan Cabbage Soup garnished with fresh parsley.

RAVIOLI & VEGETABLE SOUP

Servings: 2
Prep Time: 15 minutes
Cook Time: 20 minutes

Nutrition Info (per serving):

- Calories: 350
- Protein: 12g
- Carbohydrates: 58g
- Dietary Fiber: 8g
- Sugars: 9g
- Fat: 9g
- Saturated Fat: 2g
- Cholesterol: 15mg
- Sodium: 780mg
- Potassium: 600mg

Ingredients:

- 1 package (9 ounces) cheese or spinach ravioli

- 4 cups low-sodium vegetable broth
- 1 zucchini, diced
- 1 yellow squash, diced
- 1 red bell pepper, diced
- 1 can (14 ounces) diced tomatoes
- 1 teaspoon dried basil
- 1 teaspoon dried oregano
- Salt and pepper to taste
- Grated Parmesan cheese for garnish (optional)
- Fresh basil leaves for garnish (optional)

Directions:

1. In a big pot, bring the low-sodium vegetable broth to a boil.
2. Add the diced zucchini, yellow squash, and red bell pepper.
3. Cook for about 5 minutes or until the vegetables are slightly tender.
4. Mix the chopped tomatoes (including the liquid), dried basil, oregano, salt, and pepper.
5. Add the ravioli and cook according to package instructions until they are tender.
6. Taste and adjust the seasoning if needed.
7. Serve the pasta filled with cheese and the soup made with vegetables hot. You can add grated Parmesan cheese and fresh basil leaves on top.

SLOW-COOKER PASTA E FAGIOLI SOUP FREEZER PACK

Servings: 2 (2 portions for the freezer)
Prep Time: 20 minutes
Cook Time: 6-8 hours (slow cooker) or 30 minutes (stove-top)

Nutrition Info (per serving, prepared):

- Calories: 350
- Protein: 15g
- Carbohydrates: 60g
- Dietary Fiber: 9g
- Sugars: 10g
- Fat: 5g
- Saturated Fat: 1g
- Cholesterol: 0mg
- Sodium: 800mg
- Potassium: 800mg

Ingredients:

- 1/2 cup dried small pasta (e.g., ditalini or small shells)

- 1/2 cup cooked and drained white beans (cannellini or navy beans)
- 1/2 cup cooked and drained red kidney beans
- 1/2 cup diced tomatoes (canned or fresh)
- 1/4 cup diced carrots
- 1/4 cup diced celery
- 1/4 cup diced onion
- 1 garlic clove, minced
- 1/2 teaspoon dried oregano
- 1/2 teaspoon dried basil
- 1/4 teaspoon dried thyme
- Salt and black pepper to taste
- 2 cups vegetable broth
- Grated Parmesan cheese for serving (optional)
- Fresh basil leaves for garnish (optional)

Directions:

Preparing the Freezer Pack:

1. In a large resealable freezer bag or airtight container, combine the dried pasta, cooked white beans, cooked red kidney beans, diced tomatoes, diced carrots, diced celery, minced garlic, dried oregano, dried basil, dried thyme, salt, and black pepper. Seal the bag or container and freeze it for future use.

Cooking the Soup:

Note: This recipe makes a freezer pack for two portions of soup. To prepare the soup, follow the directions below.

Slow Cooker Method:

2. Take the frozen soup pack out of the freezer and place it in the refrigerator to thaw overnight.
3. In the morning, empty the thawed contents of the soup pack into a slow cooker.
4. Put 2 cups of vegetable broth into the slow cooker and mix it.
5. Cover and cook on **LOW** for 6-8 hours or until the pasta is tender and the flavors have melded together.
6. Before you serve the food, try a small amount to see if it needs more salt, pepper, or other spices. If it does, add more to make it taste better.

7. Serve the Slow-Cooker Pasta e Fagioli Soup with a sprinkle of grated Parmesan cheese and garnish with fresh basil leaves if desired.

Stove-Top Method:

1. Take the frozen soup pack out of the freezer and place it in a bowl of warm water to thaw for about 10-15 minutes.
2. Transfer the partially thawed soup pack to a medium-sized pot.
3. Add 2 cups of vegetable broth to the pot and stir to combine.
4. Put the cover on the pot and heat the soup medium-high until it starts boiling.
5. Once boiling, reduce the heat to low, cover, and simmer for about 30 minutes or until the pasta is tender and the soup is heated. Stir occasionally.
6. Before serving the food, try it; if necessary, add more salt, spices, or other seasonings to make it taste better.
7. Serve the Pasta e Fagioli Soup with a sprinkle of grated Parmesan cheese and garnish with fresh basil leaves if desired.

WHITE BEAN SOUP WITH TOMATO AND SHRIMP

Servings: 2
Prep Time: 15 minutes
Cook Time: 30 minutes

Nutrition Info (per serving):

- Calories: 320
- Protein: 28g
- Carbohydrates: 34g
- Dietary Fiber: 8g
- Sugars: 5g
- Fat: 8g
- Saturated Fat: 1g
- Cholesterol: 150mg
- Sodium: 540mg
- Potassium: 760mg

Ingredients:

- 1 pound large shrimp, peeled and deveined
- 1 tablespoon olive oil
- 1 onion, chopped
- 2 cloves garlic, minced
- 1 can (14 ounces) white beans, drained and rinsed
- 1 can (14 ounces) diced tomatoes
- 4 cups low-sodium vegetable broth
- 1 teaspoon dried thyme
- Salt and pepper to taste
- Fresh basil leaves for garnish (optional)

Directions:

1. In a large pot, heat the olive oil over medium heat.
2. Add the chopped onion and minced garlic. Sauté until the onion is translucent.
3. Stir in the white beans, diced tomatoes (with their juice), dried thyme, salt, and pepper.
4. Pour in the low-sodium vegetable broth and bring the soup to a simmer.
5. Add the peeled and deveined shrimp to the simmering soup and cook for about 3-5 minutes until the shrimp turn pink and opaque.
6. Taste and adjust the seasoning if needed.
7. If desired, serve the White Bean Soup with Tomato and shrimp hot, garnished with fresh basil leaves.

SHRIMP & FISH STEW

Servings: 2
Prep Time: 15 minutes
Cook Time: 25 minutes

Nutrition Info (per serving):

- Calories: 290
- Protein: 30g
- Carbohydrates: 17g
- Dietary Fiber: 3g
- Sugars: 5g
- Fat: 10g
- Saturated Fat: 2g
- Cholesterol: 160mg
- Sodium: 580mg
- Potassium: 680mg

Ingredients:

- Cut half a pound of white fish fillets (like cod or haddock) into small, manageable pieces.
- 1/2 pound large shrimp, peeled and deveined
- 1 tablespoon olive oil
- 1 onion, chopped
- 2 cloves garlic, minced
- 1 red bell pepper, diced
- 1 can (14 ounces) diced tomatoes
- 2 cups low-sodium vegetable broth
- 1 teaspoon dried basil
- 1 teaspoon dried oregano
- Salt and pepper to taste
- Fresh parsley for garnish (optional)

Directions:

1. In a large pot, heat the olive oil over medium heat.
2. Add the chopped onion and minced garlic. Sauté until the onion is translucent.
3. Add the chopped red bell pepper to the pan and cook it for 2-3 minutes.
4. Add the diced tomatoes (with their juice), dried basil, dried oregano, salt, and pepper. Cook for 5 minutes.
5. Pour in the low-sodium vegetable broth and bring the stew to a simmer.
6. Add the white fish fillets and shrimp to the simmering stew. Cook for about 5-7 minutes or until the seafood is cooked.
7. Taste and adjust the seasoning if needed.
8. Serve the Shrimp and fish Stew hot, garnished with fresh parsley if desired.

These Mediterranean diet-inspired soup recipes offer a variety of flavors and ingredients to enjoy as part of your Mediterranean-inspired meals. Enjoy these hearty and flavorful options!

WALNUT-ROSEMARY CRUSTED SALMON

Ingredients:

- 2 salmon fillets (6 ounces each)
- 1/4 cup chopped walnuts
- 1 tablespoon fresh rosemary leaves, chopped
- 1 clove garlic, minced
- 1 tablespoon whole-grain Dijon mustard
- 1/2 tablespoon lemon juice
- 1 tablespoon olive oil
- Salt and pepper to taste
- Lemon wedges for garnish (optional)

Directions:

1. Preheat your oven to 400°F (200°C). Line a baking sheet with parchment paper.
2. Combine chopped walnuts, chopped fresh rosemary, minced garlic, whole-grain Dijon mustard, lemon juice, and olive oil in a small bowl. Mix until you have a coarse paste.
3. Put the salmon pieces on the baking sheet you have prepared.
4. Season the salmon fillets with salt and pepper.

5. Spread the walnut-rosemary mixture evenly on top of each salmon fillet, pressing it down gently.
6. Bake in the oven for about 12-15 minutes until the salmon flakes easily with a fork, and the crust is golden brown.
7. Serve the Walnut-Rosemary Crusted Salmon hot, garnished with lemon wedges if desired.

CHEESY SPINACH-&-ARTICHOKE STUFFED SPAGHETTI SQUASH

Ingredients:

- 1 medium spaghetti squash
- 1 cup fresh baby spinach
- 1/2 can (7 ounces) artichoke hearts, drained and chopped
- 1/2 cup part-skim ricotta cheese
- 1/2 cup shredded mozzarella cheese
- 2 tablespoons grated Parmesan cheese
- 1 clove garlic, minced
- 1/2 teaspoon dried basil
- 1/2 teaspoon dried oregano
- Salt and pepper to taste
- Olive oil for drizzling
- Fresh basil leaves for garnish (optional)

Directions:

1. Preheat your oven to 400°F (200°C).
2. Cut the spaghetti squash into two halves from top to bottom, and remove the seeds from the inside.
3. Place the squash halves on a baking sheet cut side up.
4. Drizzle each squash half with olive oil and season with salt and pepper.
5. Roast the squash in the oven for about 40-45 minutes, or until the flesh is tender and easily separated into spaghetti-like strands with a fork.
6. While the squash is roasting, prepare the filling. In a bowl, combine chopped baby spinach, chopped artichoke hearts, ricotta cheese, shredded mozzarella cheese, grated Parmesan cheese, minced garlic, dried basil, dried oregano, salt, and pepper.
7. Once the squash is done, use a fork to scrape the flesh to create spaghetti-like strands, leaving the squash shells intact.
8. Add the spaghetti squash strands to the filling mixture and stir to combine.
9. Fill each squash shell with the cheesy spinach and artichoke mixture.
10. Return the stuffed squash halves to the oven and bake for 10-15 minutes, or until the filling is heated and the cheese is melted and bubbly.
11. Enjoy the Cheesy Spinach and Artichoke Stuffed Spaghetti Squash hot, and add fresh basil leaves on top.

SKILLET CHICKEN WITH ORZO AND TOMATOES

Ingredients:

- 2 boneless, skinless chicken breasts (6 ounces each)
- 1/2 cup whole wheat orzo pasta
- 1/2 can (7 ounces) diced tomatoes
- 1/2 onion, chopped
- 1 clove garlic, minced
- 1/2 teaspoon dried basil
- 1/2 teaspoon dried oregano
- Salt and pepper to taste
- 1 cup low-sodium chicken broth
- 2 tablespoons grated Parmesan cheese
- Fresh basil leaves for garnish (optional)

Directions:

1. Sprinkle salt, pepper, dried basil, and oregano on the chicken breasts.

2. Heat the olive oil in a skillet on medium-high heat.
3. Put the seasoned chicken breasts in the pan and cook them on each side for 4-5 minutes until they are cooked and no longer pink in the center. Remove the chicken from the skillet and set aside.
4. In the same skillet, add chopped onion and minced garlic. Sauté until the onion is translucent.
5. Stir in whole wheat orzo pasta and diced tomatoes (with their juice). Cook for 2-3 minutes.
6. Add low-salt chicken broth to the cooking pot and heat until it bubbles gently.
7. Return the cooked chicken breasts to the skillet, placing them on the orzo mixture.
8. Cover the skillet and simmer for 10-15 minutes until the orzo is cooked and the chicken is heated.
9. Sprinkle-grated Parmesan cheese over the top.
10. Garnish with fresh basil leaves if desired.
11. Serve the Skillet Chicken with Orzo and tomatoes hot.

FETA & ROASTED RED PEPPER STUFFED CHICKEN BREASTS

Servings: 2
Prep Time: 15 minutes
Cook Time: 30 minutes

Nutrition Info (per serving):

- Calories: 350
- Protein: 35g
- Carbohydrates: 4g
- Dietary Fiber: 1g
- Sugars: 2g
- Fat: 21g
- Saturated Fat: 8g
- Cholesterol: 120mg
- Sodium: 650mg
- Potassium: 470mg

Ingredients:

- 2 boneless, skinless chicken breasts (6 ounces each)
- 1/2 cup crumbled feta cheese
- 1/4 cup roasted red peppers, chopped
- 2 cloves garlic, minced
- 1 tablespoon fresh basil leaves, chopped
- 1 tablespoon fresh oregano leaves, chopped
- Salt and pepper to taste
- 1 tablespoon olive oil
- 1/2 cup low-sodium chicken broth
- 1/4 cup dry white wine (optional)
- Lemon wedges for garnish (optional)
- Fresh basil or oregano leaves for garnish (optional)

Directions:

1. Preheat your oven to 375°F (190°C).
2. Combine crumbled feta cheese, chopped roasted red peppers, minced garlic, fresh basil, fresh oregano, salt, and pepper in a small bowl. Mix until the ingredients are well combined.
3. Put the chicken breasts on a clean surface. Using a sharp knife, make a horizontal slit along the side of each chicken breast to create a pocket without cutting through.
4. Stuff each chicken breast pocket with the feta and roasted red pepper mixture, dividing it evenly between the breasts. Squeeze the sides of the chicken together to close the openings.
5. Season the outside of the chicken breasts with a little more salt and pepper.
6. In an oven-safe skillet, heat olive oil over medium-high heat.
7. Put the stuffed chicken breasts in the frying pan and cook them on each side for 2-3 minutes.
8. If using, pour the dry white wine and allow it to cook for a minute or two until it reduces slightly.
9. Add the low-sodium chicken broth to the skillet.
10. Put the pan in the hot oven and cook for 15-20 minutes until the chicken is finished cooking and reaches a temperature of 165°F (74°C).
11. Remove the skillet from the oven and let the chicken rest for a few minutes.
12. Garnish with lemon wedges and fresh basil or oregano leaves, if desired.

13. Serve the Feta and roasted Red Pepper Stuffed Chicken Breasts hot with your favorite Mediterranean side dishes or a fresh salad.

CHARRED SHRIMP, PESTO & QUINOA BOWLS

Servings: 2
Prep Time: 15 minutes
Cook Time: 15 minutes

Nutrition Info (per serving):

- Calories: 420
- Protein: 28g
- Carbohydrates: 36g
- Dietary Fiber: 4g
- Sugars: 2g
- Fat: 18g
- Saturated Fat: 3g
- Cholesterol: 150mg
- Sodium: 520mg
- Potassium: 620mg

Ingredients:

For the Pesto:

- 2 cups fresh basil leaves, packed
- 1/4 cup grated Parmesan cheese
- 1/4 cup pine nuts, toasted
- 2 cloves garlic, minced
- 1/2 cup extra-virgin olive oil
- Salt and pepper to taste

For the Quinoa Bowls:

- 1 cup quinoa, rinsed and drained
- 1 3/4 cups water
- 1 pound large shrimp, peeled and deveined
- 1 tablespoon olive oil
- Salt and pepper to taste
- 2 cups cherry tomatoes, halved
- 2 cups baby arugula
- Lemon wedges for garnish (optional)

Directions:

For the Pesto:

1. Combine fresh basil leaves, grated Parmesan cheese, toasted pine nuts, and minced garlic in a food processor.
2. Pulse until the ingredients are finely chopped.
3. Gradually pour the extra-virgin olive oil into the food processor while it is running until the pesto becomes the consistency you like.
4. Season the pesto with salt and pepper to taste. Set aside.

For the Quinoa Bowls:

1. In a medium-sized saucepan, mix quinoa and water. Heat it until it starts bubbling.
2. Turn the heat down low, cover the pot, and let it cook gently for around 15 minutes or until the quinoa is fully cooked and has soaked up all the water. Remove from heat and let it sit, covered, for 5 minutes. Fluff with a fork.
3. While the quinoa is cooking, season the shrimp with salt and pepper.

4. In a large skillet, heat olive oil over medium-high heat.
5. Put the shrimp prepared with spices into the cooking pan and cook it for 2-3 minutes on each side until it becomes not see-through and is fully cooked.
6. Remove the cooked shrimp from the skillet and set aside.
7. Add halved cherry tomatoes in the same skillet and cook for 3-4 minutes until they soften and char slightly.
8. Put equal amounts of cooked quinoa into two bowls to make the bowls.
9. Top with baby arugula, charred cherry tomatoes, and cooked shrimp.
10. Drizzle the freshly made pesto over the top of each bowl.
11. Garnish with lemon wedges if desired.
12. Serve the Charred Shrimp, Pesto, and quinoa Bowls hot, and enjoy this flavorful and nutritious Mediterranean-inspired meal!

SHEET-PAN SALMON WITH SWEET POTATOES AND BROCCOLI

Servings: 2
Prep Time: 15 minutes
Cook Time: 25 minutes

Nutrition Info (per serving):

- Calories: 380
- Protein: 30g
- Carbohydrates: 35g
- Dietary Fiber: 6g
- Sugars: 9g
- Fat: 14g
- Saturated Fat: 2g
- Cholesterol: 75mg
- Sodium: 350mg
- Potassium: 1050mg

Ingredients:

- 2 salmon fillets (6 ounces each)
- 2 cups sweet potatoes, peeled and cubed
- 2 cups broccoli florets
- 2 tablespoons olive oil
- 2 cloves garlic, minced
- 1 teaspoon dried thyme
- 1 teaspoon dried rosemary
- Salt and pepper to taste
- Lemon wedges for garnish (optional)

Directions:

1. Preheat your oven to 400°F (200°C). Line a large baking sheet with parchment paper.
2. Combine the cubed sweet potatoes, broccoli florets, minced garlic, dried thyme, rosemary, olive oil, salt, and pepper in a mixing bowl. Mix the vegetables with the seasoning and oil until they are covered.
3. Put the seasoned sweet potatoes and broccoli on the baking sheet in a flat layer.
4. Place the salmon fillets on the baking sheet, skin side down, nestled among the vegetables.
5. Put the salmon and sweet potatoes in the oven and cook for about 20-25 minutes. The salmon is done when cooked through and easily breaks apart with a fork, and the sweet potatoes should be soft and have a slightly sweet taste.
6. If desired, garnish with lemon wedges before serving.
7. Serve the Sheet-Pan Salmon with Sweet Potatoes and broccoli hot, and enjoy this wholesome and easy-to-make meal!

SPINACH RAVIOLI WITH ARTICHOKES AND OLIVES

Servings: 2
Prep Time: 10 minutes
Cook Time: 15 minutes

Nutrition Info (per serving):

- Calories: 450
- Protein: 16g
- Carbohydrates: 47g
- Dietary Fiber: 9g
- Sugars: 2g
- Fat: 22g
- Saturated Fat: 4g
- Cholesterol: 40mg
- Sodium: 600mg
- Potassium: 300mg

Ingredients:

- 9 ounces spinach and cheese ravioli (fresh or frozen)
- 2 tablespoons olive oil
- 2 cloves garlic, minced
- 1 can (14 ounces) artichoke hearts, drained and quartered
- 1/2 cup pitted Kalamata olives, sliced
- 1/4 cup sun-dried tomatoes, chopped
- 1/4 cup fresh basil leaves, chopped
- 1/4 cup grated Parmesan cheese
- Salt and pepper to taste
- Red pepper flakes (optional for added heat)

Directions:

1. Cook the spinach and cheese ravioli according to the package instructions. Drain and set aside.
2. In a big frying pan, warm the olive oil on medium heat.
3. Add the minced garlic to the skillet and sauté for about 1 minute or until fragrant.
4. Add the quartered artichoke hearts to the skillet and cook for 3-4 minutes until golden brown.
5. Stir in the sliced Kalamata olives and chopped sun-dried tomatoes. Cook for an additional 2 minutes.
6. Add the cooked spinach and cheese ravioli to the skillet and gently toss to combine with the artichokes, olives, and sun-dried tomatoes. Cook for 2-3 minutes to heat through.
7. Stir in the chopped fresh basil and grated Parmesan cheese. Season with salt and pepper to taste. If you like a bit of heat, add red pepper flakes at this stage.
8. Serve the Spinach Ravioli with Artichokes and olives hot, garnished with extra grated Parmesan cheese and fresh basil leaves if desired.
9. Enjoy this Mediterranean-inspired pasta dish with a burst of flavors!

CAULIFLOWER RICE BOWLS WITH GRILLED CHICKEN

Servings: 2
Prep Time: 20 minutes
Cook Time: 20 minutes

Nutrition Info (per serving):

- Calories: 350
- Protein: 30g
- Carbohydrates: 12g
- Dietary Fiber: 5g
- Sugars: 4g
- Fat: 18g
- Saturated Fat: 3g
- Cholesterol: 75mg
- Sodium: 600mg
- Potassium: 700mg

Ingredients:

<u>For the Grilled Chicken:</u>

- 2 boneless, skinless chicken breasts (6 ounces each)
- 1 tablespoon olive oil
- 1 teaspoon dried oregano
- Salt and pepper to taste
- Lemon wedges for garnish (optional)

<u>For the Cauliflower Rice:</u>

- 1 medium head of cauliflower, cut into florets
- 2 tablespoons olive oil
- 2 cloves garlic, minced
- Salt and pepper to taste

<u>For the Toppings:</u>

- 1 cup cherry tomatoes, halved
- 1/2 cucumber, diced
- 1/4 cup red onion, finely chopped
- 1/4 cup fresh parsley, chopped
- 1/4 cup feta cheese, crumbled
- Tzatziki sauce for drizzling (optional)

Directions:

<u>For the Grilled Chicken:</u>

1. Mix olive oil, dried oregano, salt, and pepper in a small bowl.
2. Brush the chicken breasts with the olive oil and coat both sides evenly.
3. Preheat your grill or grill pan over medium-high heat. Grill the chicken for about 6-7 minutes on each side or until they are cooked through and have nice grill marks. The internal temperature should reach 165°F (74°C).
4. Remove the grilled chicken from the heat and let it rest for a few minutes before slicing it into strips. Squeeze fresh lemon juice over the top if desired.

<u>For the Cauliflower Rice:</u>

1. Place the cauliflower florets in a food processor and pulse until they resemble rice grains. You may need to do this in batches.

2. In a large skillet, heat olive oil over medium-high heat. Add minced garlic and sauté for about 30 seconds or until fragrant.
3. Add the cauliflower rice to the skillet and cook for 5-7 minutes, stirring occasionally until tender and slightly golden. Season with salt and pepper to taste.

To Assemble the Bowls:

1. Divide the cauliflower rice between two serving bowls.
2. Top the cauliflower rice with sliced grilled chicken.
3. Add cherry tomatoes, diced cucumber, chopped red onion, and fresh parsley.
4. Sprinkle crumbled feta cheese over the bowls.
5. Drizzle with tzatziki sauce, if desired.
6. Serve the Cauliflower Rice Bowls with Grilled Chicken and enjoy this healthy and satisfying Mediterranean-inspired meal!

PROSCIUTTO PIZZA WITH CORN & ARUGULA

Servings: 2
Prep Time: 15 minutes
Cook Time: 15 minutes

Nutrition Info (per serving, for 4 servings):

- Calories: 330
- Protein: 14g
- Carbohydrates: 36g
- Dietary Fiber: 2g
- Sugars: 1g
- Fat: 15g
- Saturated Fat: 6g
- Cholesterol: 25mg
- Sodium: 610mg
- Potassium: 160mg

Ingredients:

- 1 pound pizza dough (store-bought or homemade)
- 1/4 cup pizza sauce
- 1 1/2 cups shredded mozzarella cheese

- 4 slices prosciutto
- 1/2 cup corn kernels (fresh or frozen)
- 1 cup fresh arugula
- 1/4 cup grated Parmesan cheese
- 1 tablespoon olive oil
- You can add crushed red pepper flakes to make it spicier.

Directions:

1. Preheat your oven to 475°F (245°C). If you have a pizza stone, place it in the oven while it's preheating.
2. Spread the pizza dough to your preferred thickness on a surface covered with flour.
3. Move the flattened dough onto a special paddle for pizza or a regular baking sheet that is upside down, and sprinkle some cornmeal or flour on it.
4. Spread the pizza sauce evenly over the dough, leaving a small border for the crust.
5. Sprinkle the shredded mozzarella cheese over the sauce.
6. Tear the prosciutto slices into smaller pieces and distribute them over the cheese.
7. Scatter the corn kernels evenly over the pizza.
8. Transfer the pizza to the preheated oven (or onto the pizza stone if you're using one) and bake for about 12-15 minutes until the crust is golden and the cheese is bubbly and slightly browned.
9. While the pizza is baking, toss the fresh arugula with olive oil in a bowl.
10. After the pizza finishes cooking, take it out of the oven and quickly spread the arugula on top.
11. Sprinkle the grated Parmesan cheese and, if desired, crushed red pepper flakes over the arugula.
12. Slice and serve the Prosciutto Pizza with Corn and arugula hot. Enjoy your homemade pizza!

This pizza offers a wonderful combination of flavors: corn's sweetness, prosciutto's saltiness, and arugula's peppery freshness.

EATINGWELL'S EGGPLANT PARMESAN

Servings: 2
Prep Time: 30 minutes
Cook Time: 50 minutes

Nutrition Info (per serving):

- Calories: 340
- Protein: 17g
- Carbohydrates: 30g
- Dietary Fiber: 7g
- Sugars: 9g
- Fat: 18g
- Saturated Fat: 5g
- Cholesterol: 12mg
- Sodium: 760mg
- Potassium: 530mg

Ingredients:

- 1 large eggplant (about 1 pound), sliced into 1/2-inch rounds
- 1 cup whole-wheat breadcrumbs

- 1/4 cup grated Parmesan cheese
- 1/4 cup chopped fresh basil
- 1/2 teaspoon salt, divided
- 1/4 teaspoon ground pepper
- 1 cup all-purpose flour
- 3 large eggs, beaten
- 3 cups tomato sauce (store-bought or homemade)
- 1 1/2 cups shredded mozzarella cheese
- 2 tablespoons olive oil
- Fresh basil leaves for garnish (optional)

Directions:

1. Turn on your oven and set it to 375 degrees Fahrenheit (190 degrees Celsius) before cooking. Spray cooking oil on a baking sheet.
2. Put the slices of eggplant on the baking sheet that has been prepared. Sprinkle a small amount of salt, around 1/4 teaspoon, over the food. Leave it for approximately 15 minutes without disturbing it. Use paper towels to remove any moisture from the eggplant slices by gently pressing them.
3. Combine whole-wheat breadcrumbs, grated Parmesan cheese, chopped fresh basil, ground pepper, and the remaining 1/4 teaspoon of salt in a shallow dish.
4. Place all-purpose flour in another shallow dish and beaten eggs in a third shallow dish.
5. Coat each slice of eggplant in flour, removing any extra. Put it in the egg mixture, let the extra drip off, and then cover it with the breadcrumbs. Take the breadcrumbs and stick them onto the eggplant.
6. Put the breaded eggplant slices on the baking sheet that is ready for use.
7. Bake in the oven for about 20-25 minutes or until the eggplant is tender and the breadcrumbs are golden brown.
8. While the eggplant is cooking in the oven, put 1 cup of tomato sauce on the bottom of a large baking dish that is 9x13 inches in size.
9. After baking the eggplant, take it out of the oven. After that, increase the oven's heat to 400°F (200°C).
10. Put half of the cooked eggplant slices in the baking dish.
11. Top with half the remaining tomato sauce and half the shredded mozzarella cheese.
12. Add the remaining eggplant slices and cover with tomato sauce and mozzarella cheese.
13. Drizzle olive oil over the top of the dish.

14. Put it in the hot oven for around 20-25 minutes or until the cheese has melted and bubbled.
15. Garnish with fresh basil leaves if desired.
16. Serve the Eggplant Parmesan hot. Enjoy your homemade, healthier version of this classic Italian dish!

BBQ SHRIMP WITH GARLICKY KALE & PARMESAN-HERB COUSCOUS

Servings: 2
Prep Time: 20 minutes
Cook Time: 20 minutes

Nutrition Info (per serving):

- Calories: 420
- Protein: 30g
- Carbohydrates: 45g
- Dietary Fiber: 5g
- Sugars: 3g
- Fat: 12g
- Saturated Fat: 3g
- Cholesterol: 150mg
- Sodium: 700mg
- Potassium: 550mg

Ingredients:

<u>For the BBQ Shrimp:</u>

- 12 large shrimp, peeled and deveined
- 2 tablespoons BBQ sauce (your favorite variety)
- 1 tablespoon olive oil
- 1/2 teaspoon smoked paprika
- Salt and pepper to taste
- Lemon wedges for garnish (optional)

<u>For the Garlicky Kale:</u>

- Cut up 2 cups of fresh kale by removing the stems and chopping it.
- 2 cloves garlic, minced
- 1 tablespoon olive oil
- Salt and pepper to taste
- Red pepper flakes (optional for added heat)

<u>For the Parmesan-Herb Couscous:</u>

- 1 cup couscous
- 1 cup chicken or vegetable broth
- 2 tablespoons grated Parmesan cheese
- 1 tablespoon fresh herbs (such as parsley, basil, or chives), chopped
- Salt and pepper to taste

Directions:

<u>For the BBQ Shrimp:</u>

1. Combine BBQ sauce, olive oil, smoked paprika, salt, and pepper in a bowl.
2. Add the peeled and deveined shrimp to the bowl and toss to coat them in the BBQ sauce mixture.
3. Preheat a grill or grill pan over medium-high heat. Grill the shrimp on each side for 2-3 minutes.
4. Remove the grilled BBQ shrimp from the heat and set them aside. If you want to, you can put fresh lemon juice on the shrimp to make it taste better.

<u>For the Garlicky Kale:</u>

1. In a large skillet, heat olive oil over medium heat.
2. Add minced garlic and sauté for about 30 seconds or until fragrant.
3. Add the chopped kale to the skillet and cook for about 3-4 minutes, until the kale is wilted and slightly tender. Add salt, pepper, and red pepper flakes (optional)

For the Parmesan-Herb Couscous:

1. In a saucepan, bring chicken or vegetable broth to a boil.
2. Mix the couscous with the other ingredients, put a lid on it, and take it off the stove. Leave it alone for approximately 5 minutes.
3. Fluff the cooked couscous with a fork and add grated Parmesan cheese and fresh herbs. Season with salt and pepper to taste.

To Assemble the Dish:

1. Divide the Parmesan-Herb Couscous between two serving plates.
2. Top the couscous with the Garlicky Kale.
3. Arrange the BBQ Shrimp on top of the kale.
4. Garnish with lemon wedges if desired.
5. Serve the BBQ Shrimp with Garlicky Kale & Parmesan-Herb Couscous hot. Enjoy this flavorful and balanced meal for two!

ONE-SKILLET SALMON WITH FENNEL AND SUN-DRIED TOMATO COUSCOUS

Servings: 2
Prep Time: 15 minutes
Cook Time: 25 minutes

Nutrition Info (per serving):

- Calories: 480
- Protein: 32g
- Carbohydrates: 50g
- Dietary Fiber: 6g
- Sugars: 6g
- Fat: 18g
- Saturated Fat: 3g
- Cholesterol: 60mg
- Sodium: 720mg
- Potassium: 820mg

Ingredients:

<u>For the Salmon:</u>

- 2 salmon fillets (6 ounces each)
- 1 tablespoon olive oil
- Salt and pepper to taste
- 1 lemon, sliced (for garnish)

<u>For the Sun-Dried Tomato Couscous:</u>

- 1 cup couscous
- 1 cup chicken or vegetable broth
- 1/4 cup sun-dried tomatoes, chopped
- 1/4 cup fennel bulb, thinly sliced
- 2 cloves garlic, minced
- 1 tablespoon olive oil
- 1/2 teaspoon dried oregano
- Salt and pepper to taste
- Fresh parsley leaves for garnish (optional)

Directions:

<u>For the Salmon:</u>

1. Preheat your oven to 400°F (200°C).
2. Season the salmon fillets with salt and pepper.
3. Heat one tablespoon of olive oil in a skillet that can be used in the oven on medium-high heat.
4. Place the seasoned salmon fillets in the skillet, skin side down. Sear for 2-3 minutes until the skin is crispy and golden.
5. Flip the salmon fillets and transfer the skillet to the preheated oven.
6. Roast in the oven for 10-12 minutes or until the salmon is cooked and flakes easily with a fork.
7. While the salmon is cooking, you can prepare the Sun-Dried Tomato Couscous.

<u>For the Sun-Dried Tomato Couscous:</u>

1. In a saucepan, bring chicken or vegetable broth to a boil.

2. Stir in the couscous, cover with a lid, and remove from heat. Let it sit for about 5 minutes.
3. Fluff the cooked couscous using a fork and put it to the side.
4. Heat 1 tablespoon of olive oil over medium heat in a separate skillet.
5. Add minced garlic, thinly sliced fennel, and chopped sun-dried tomatoes to the skillet. Sauté for about 3-4 minutes, or until the fennel softens and the garlic is fragrant.
6. Stir in dried oregano, salt, and pepper.

To Assemble the Dish:

1. Divide the Sun-Dried Tomato Couscous between two serving plates.
2. Place the roasted salmon fillets on top of the couscous.
3. If you want, you can decorate it with lemon slices and fresh parsley leaves.
4. Serve the One-Skillet Salmon with Fennel and sun-dried Tomato Couscous hot. Enjoy this flavorful and nutritious meal for two!

CHICKEN & SPINACH SKILLET PASTA WITH LEMON & PARMESAN

Servings: 2
Prep Time: 15 minutes
Cook Time: 20 minutes

Nutrition Info (per serving):

- Calories: 480
- Protein: 28g
- Carbohydrates: 58g
- Dietary Fiber: 4g
- Sugars: 3g
- Fat: 15g
- Saturated Fat: 5g
- Cholesterol: 70mg
- Sodium: 430mg
- Potassium: 350mg

Ingredients:

- 4 ounces penne pasta (or your favorite pasta)
- Two chicken breasts without bones or skin, weighing 6 ounces each.
- Salt and pepper to taste
- 1 tablespoon olive oil
- 2 cloves garlic, minced
- 2 cups fresh spinach leaves
- 1 lemon, zest and juice
- 1/4 cup grated Parmesan cheese
- 2 tablespoons fresh basil leaves, chopped (optional)
- Red pepper flakes (optional for added heat)

Directions:

1. Boil the penne pasta as per the instructions on the package until it is cooked but still firm to bite. Empty it and put it to the side.
2. While the pasta is being cooked, add salt and pepper to the chicken breasts to add flavor.
3. In a large skillet, heat olive oil over medium-high heat. Put the chicken breasts in and cook them for about 6-7 minutes on each side until they are fully cooked and don't have any pink in the middle. The inside of the food needs to be heated up to 165°F (74°C).
4. Take the cooked chicken out of the skillet and let it sit for a little while. Next, cut it into thin pieces.
5. In the same pan, put in minced garlic and cook for about 30 seconds or until it smells good.
6. Put fresh spinach leaves in the skillet and cook for 1-2 minutes or until they become soft and shrink in size.
7. Return the sliced chicken to the skillet and add the cooked penne pasta. Toss everything together.
8. Grate the lemon peel and press the juice onto the pasta and chicken mixture. Mix everything.
9. Stir in grated Parmesan cheese until it's well incorporated and creates a creamy sauce.
10. Add chopped fresh basil leaves for extra flavor and a pinch of red pepper flakes for added heat if desired.
11. Try the food and add salt, pepper, or lemon juice if it tastes bad.

12. Serve the Chicken and spinach Skillet Pasta with Lemon and parmesan hot. Enjoy this delicious and zesty meal for two!

This dish combines tender chicken, fresh spinach, and zesty lemon with creamy Parmesan for a flavorful and satisfying pasta dinner.

Chapter 6:
Desserts and Sweets for Two

OLIVE OIL YOGURT BUNDT CAKE

Servings: 2
Prep Time: 15 minutes
Cook Time: 30-35 minutes

Nutrition Info (per serving):

- Calories: 350
- Protein: 6g
- Carbohydrates: 34g
- Dietary Fiber: 1g
- Sugars: 20g
- Fat: 22g
- Saturated Fat: 4g
- Cholesterol: 80mg
- Sodium: 180mg
- Potassium: 90mg

Ingredients:

- 1/2 cup all-purpose flour
- 1/4 teaspoon baking powder
- 1/8 teaspoon baking soda
- Pinch of salt
- 1/4 cup granulated sugar
- 1/4 cup plain yogurt
- 1/4 cup extra-virgin olive oil
- 1/2 teaspoon vanilla extract
- Zest of half a lemon (optional)
- 1 egg

Directions:

1. Turn on your oven and set the temperature to 350°F (175°C). Grease a small Bundt cake pan or a mini Bundt cake pan (about 4 inches in diameter) with olive oil or cooking spray.
2. Mix the flour, baking powder, baking soda, and a little salt in a small bowl. Keep the dry mixture in a separate place.
3. In a separate bowl, combine the granulated sugar, plain yogurt, extra-virgin olive oil, vanilla extract, and lemon zest (if using). Mix until well combined.
4. Mix the egg into the wet mixture and whisk it until completely combined.
5. Slowly pour the dry mixture into the wet mixture until you have a silky cake batter.
6. Pour the batter into the greased Bundt cake pan.
7. Put the food in the oven heating up, and leave it there for 30-35 minutes. To determine if it's cooked, insert a toothpick into the center. If it comes out without any crumbs or with only a few on it, then it's done.
8. Take the cake out of the oven and allow it to cool in the pan for approximately 10 minutes.
9. Carefully slide a knife around the sides of the cake to make it easier to remove, then flip it onto a plate for serving.
10. Allow the Olive Oil Yogurt Bundt Cake to cool completely before serving.
11. You can sprinkle powdered sugar on the cake after it cools down or put a sugary sauce made with powdered sugar and lemon juice on top for extra sweetness (if you want).
12. Slice and enjoy your homemade Olive Oil Yogurt Bundt Cake!

This cake is moist and slightly tangy from the yogurt, with a delightful olive oil flavor. It's a perfect treat for two!

GREEK YOGURT BARK WITH BERRIES

Servings: 2
Prep Time: 10 minutes
Freeze Time: 2-3 hours

Nutrition Info (per serving):

- Calories: 150
- Protein: 10g
- Carbohydrates: 23g
- Dietary Fiber: 3g
- Sugars: 15g
- Fat: 2g
- Saturated Fat: 0g
- Cholesterol: 3mg
- Sodium: 30mg
- Potassium: 280mg

Ingredients:

- 1 cup Greek yogurt (plain or vanilla)
- 2 tablespoons honey or maple syrup
- 1/2 teaspoon vanilla extract (optional)
- 1/4 cup granola (your choice of flavor)

- 1/4 cup mixed berries (e.g., strawberries, blueberries, raspberries)

Directions:

1. Combine the Greek yogurt, honey (or maple syrup), and vanilla extract in a mixing bowl. Mix until well combined.
2. Cover a little baking sheet or tray with parchment paper.
3. Pour the Greek yogurt mixture onto the parchment paper, spreading it evenly to about 1/4-inch thickness.
4. Sprinkle the granola evenly over the yogurt.
5. Scatter the mixed berries on top of the granola, pressing them gently into the yogurt mixture.
6. Place the baking sheet or tray in the freezer and let it freeze for 2-3 hours or until the yogurt bark is completely firm.
7. Once frozen, remove the Greek Yogurt Bark with Berries from the freezer.
8. Use a knife or your hands to break the bark into small pieces or irregular shards.
9. Serve the yogurt bark immediately as a refreshing and healthy snack for two.
10. Enjoy your homemade Greek Yogurt bar with Berries!

DOUBLE CHOCOLATE STRAWBERRY COCONUT BROWNIES

Servings: 2
Prep Time: 10 minutes
Cook Time: 20-25 minutes

Nutrition Info (per serving):

- Calories: 380
- Protein: 4g
- Carbohydrates: 44g
- Dietary Fiber: 3g
- Sugars: 29g
- Fat: 22g
- Saturated Fat: 13g
- Cholesterol: 70mg
- Sodium: 160mg
- Potassium: 180mg

Ingredients:

- 1/4 cup unsalted butter (1/2 stick)
- 1/2 cup granulated sugar
- 1/4 cup cocoa powder
- 1/4 teaspoon salt
- 1/2 teaspoon vanilla extract
- 1 large egg
- 1/4 cup all-purpose flour
- 1/4 cup semi-sweet chocolate chips
- 1/4 cup strawberries, diced
- 2 tablespoons shredded coconut (sweetened or unsweetened)

Directions:

1. Turn on your oven and set it to 350 degrees Fahrenheit (175 degrees Celsius) before cooking. Cover a small baking pan or dish (approximately 6x6 inches) with parchment paper after greasing it.
2. In a safe bowl to put in the microwave, heat the unsalted butter for around 30 seconds until it completely melts.
3. Mix the granulated sugar, cocoa powder, and salt into the melted butter until everything is well.
4. Add the vanilla extract and the egg to the mixture and whisk until the batter is smooth and glossy.
5. Gently fold in the all-purpose flour until just incorporated.
6. Stir in the semi-sweet chocolate chips, diced strawberries, and shredded coconut. Stir until the ingredients are spread evenly throughout the batter.
7. Put the brownie mixture into the baking pan that has been prepared, making sure to spread it out evenly.
8. Put the dish in the oven that has been heated beforehand and leave it there for about 20 to 25 minutes. You can check if it's done by sticking a toothpick into the middle, and if it comes out with a few moist crumbs, it's ready. Make sure you don't bake for too long.
9. Take the brownies out of the oven and wait for them to cool in the pan for around 10 minutes.
10. Carefully lift the brownies from the pan using the parchment paper overhang and transfer them to a cutting board.
11. Cut the brownies into two portions and cool completely before serving.

12. Have fun eating your homemade brownies with chocolate, strawberry, and coconut flavors. You can have them with milk or ice cream.

NO-SUGAR-ADDED MINI APPLE PIES

Servings: 2
Prep Time: 15 minutes
Cook Time: 30-35 minutes

Nutrition Info (per serving):

- Calories: 220
- Protein: 3g
- Carbohydrates: 41g
- Dietary Fiber: 6g
- Sugars: 20g
- Fat: 7g
- Saturated Fat: 2g

- Cholesterol: 0mg
- Sodium: 130mg
- Potassium: 280mg

Ingredients:

For the Pie Filling:

- 2 medium-sized apples (such as Granny Smith or Honeycrisp), peeled, cored, and thinly sliced
- 1/2 teaspoon ground cinnamon
- 1/4 teaspoon ground nutmeg
- 1/4 teaspoon vanilla extract
- 1 tablespoon lemon juice

For the Pie Crust:

- 1/2 cup all-purpose flour
- 1/4 teaspoon salt
- 1/4 cup unsalted butter (1/2 stick), cold and cubed
- 2-3 tablespoons ice-cold water

Directions:

For the Pie Filling:

1. Combine the sliced apples, ground cinnamon, ground nutmeg, vanilla extract, and lemon juice in a bowl. Mix the apples until they are covered with spices and lemon juice invariably. Put away or save for later.

For the Pie Crust:

1. Mix the flour and salt in a bowl.
2. Add the cold, cubed, unsalted butter to the flour mixture.
3. To make the butter and flour mixture look like small lumps, use a pastry cutter or your hands to mix them.
4. Slowly pour in the ice-cold water, one tablespoon at a time, and stir until the dough sticks together. Be cautious not to mix too much.
5. Make the dough round. Put plastic wrap on top and place it in the fridge for 15 minutes.

To Assemble the Mini Apple Pies:

1. Turn your oven to 375°F (190°C) before using it. Grease two ramekins or mini pie dishes.
2. Remove the chilled pie dough from the refrigerator and roll it out on a lightly floured surface into a circle large enough to cover the base and sides of each ramekin.
3. Carefully line each greased ramekin with the rolled-out pie crust.
4. Divide the prepared apple filling between the two ramekins, mounding it slightly.
5. Roll out the remaining pie dough and cut it into strips. Create a lattice pattern over the tops of the mini pies by placing the strips of dough diagonally across the filling.
6. Remove any extra dough and press the edges together to close the pies tightly.
7. If desired, brush the top of each pie with a little milk for a golden finish.
8. Place the little apple pies on a flat baking sheet and bake them in the oven for 30-35 minutes. Take them out when the crust turns golden brown and the filling bubbles.
9. Remove the pies from the oven and let them cool for a few minutes before serving.
10. Serve the No-Sugar-Added Mini Apple Pies warm or at room temperature. Enjoy your homemade, healthier apple pies!

HOMEMADE BAKLAVA

Servings: 2
Prep Time: 20 minutes
Cook Time: 40 minutes

Nutrition Info (per serving):

- Calories: 400
- Protein: 5g
- Carbohydrates: 40g
- Dietary Fiber: 3g
- Sugars: 25g
- Fat: 25g
- Saturated Fat: 9g
- Cholesterol: 30mg
- Sodium: 150mg
- Potassium: 120mg

Ingredients:

- 1/2 cup unsalted butter (1 stick)
- 1 cup mixed nuts (such as walnuts, pistachios, and almonds), finely chopped
- 1/4 cup granulated sugar
- 1/2 teaspoon ground cinnamon
- 1/4 teaspoon ground cloves
- 4 sheets phyllo dough, thawed if frozen
- 1/4 cup honey
- 1/4 cup water
- 1/4 teaspoon vanilla extract
- Zest of half a lemon (optional)

Directions:

1. Turn on your oven and set the temperature to 350°F (175°C). Spread melted butter on a small baking dish or pan approximately 6x6 inches.
2. Combine the finely chopped mixed nuts, granulated sugar, ground cinnamon, and ground cloves in a mixing bowl. Mix well to distribute the spices evenly.
3. Place one sheet of phyllo dough into the greased baking dish. Take the pastry brush and apply melted butter to it. Then, spread the butter onto the thing's surface using the brush.
4. Add another sheet of phyllo dough to the first, and brush it with melted butter.
5. Continue this layering process, brushing each sheet with melted butter until you have used all four sheets of phyllo dough.
6. Sprinkle the nut mixture evenly over the layered phyllo dough.
7. Slice the baklava into either square or diamond shapes using a sharp knife.
8. Bake in the oven for about 40 minutes or until the baklava is golden brown and crisp.
9. While the sweet pastry called baklava is in the oven, get the syrup ready. In a saucepan, combine the honey, water, vanilla extract, and lemon zest (if using). Heat the mixture until it starts bubbling, then lower the temperature and let it cook slowly for around 10 minutes or until it becomes a little thicker.
10. After baking the baklava, remove it from the oven and pour the hot syrup evenly over it immediately. Allow the baklava to cool completely in the pan.
11. Once cooled, carefully remove the individual pieces and serve.
12. Enjoy your Homemade Baklava! It's a sweet and nutty treat with layers of flaky phyllo dough and a fragrant honey syrup.

MEDITERRANEAN DIET BAKED APPLE PIES

Servings: 2
Prep Time: 20 minutes
Cook Time: 30 minutes

Nutrition Info (per serving):

- Calories: 260
- Protein: 2g
- Carbohydrates: 55g
- Dietary Fiber: 6g
- Sugars: 35g
- Fat: 4g
- Saturated Fat: 1g
- Cholesterol: 0mg
- Sodium: 130mg
- Potassium: 240mg

Ingredients:

For the Apple Filling:

- 2 medium-sized apples (such as Granny Smith or Honeycrisp), peeled, cored, and diced
- 1 tablespoon honey or maple syrup
- 1/2 teaspoon ground cinnamon
- 1/4 teaspoon ground nutmeg
- 1/4 teaspoon vanilla extract
- Zest of half a lemon (optional)

For the Pie Crust:

- 1 sheet whole wheat or whole grain pie crust (store-bought or homemade)
- Olive oil or cooking spray for greasing

Directions:

For the Apple Filling:

1. In a mixing bowl, combine the diced apples, honey (or maple syrup), ground cinnamon, ground nutmeg, vanilla extract, and lemon zest (if using). Toss until the apples are well coated with the mixture. Set aside.

For the Pie Crust:

1. Preheat your oven to 375°F (190°C). Grease two small ramekins or pie dishes.
2. Roll out the whole wheat or whole grain pie crust on a lightly floured surface.
3. Slice the pie crust into two round shapes. Make sure each one is a little bit bigger than the size of your ramekins.

To Assemble the Mediterranean Diet Baked Apple Pies:

1. Place one pie crust circle into the bottom of each greased ramekin, allowing any excess to hang over the edges.
2. Divide the prepared apple filling evenly between the two ramekins, mounding the apples slightly.
3. Fold the excess pie crust over the top of the apples, creating a rustic, free-form edge.
4. If you want, put olive oil or cooking spray on the top of each pie to make it look golden.
5. Put the small bowls on a baking tray and cook them in the oven for around 30 minutes until the pastry is golden brown and the apples are soft.
6. Remove the baked apple pies from the oven and let them cool for a few minutes before serving.
7. Serve the Mediterranean Diet Baked Apple Pies warm. Enjoy this healthier twist on a classic dessert!

GREEK SYRUP-SOAKED CUSTARD PASTRY

Servings: 2
Prep Time: 15 minutes
Cook Time: 30 minutes

Nutrition Info (per serving):

- Calories: 320
- Protein: 6g
- Carbohydrates: 47g
- Dietary Fiber: 1g
- Sugars: 32g
- Fat: 12g
- Saturated Fat: 6g
- Cholesterol: 105mg
- Sodium: 160mg
- Potassium: 100mg

Ingredients:

<u>For the Custard Filling:</u>

- 1/2 cup whole milk
- 2 tablespoons granulated sugar
- 1/4 teaspoon vanilla extract
- 1 large egg
- 1 tablespoon all-purpose flour

<u>For the Pastry:</u>

- 4 sheets phyllo dough, thawed if frozen
- 2 tablespoons unsalted butter, melted
- 1/4 cup chopped walnuts or almonds (optional)

<u>For the Syrup:</u>

- 1/4 cup granulated sugar
- 1/4 cup water
- 1/2 teaspoon lemon juice
- 1/2 teaspoon orange zest (optional)
- 1/4 teaspoon ground cinnamon
- 1/4 teaspoon vanilla extract

Directions:

<u>For the Custard Filling:</u>

1. Warm the full drain in a pan over medium warm until it's warm but not bubbling. Evacuate it from the warm and set it aside.
2. In an isolated bowl, whisk together the granulated sugar, vanilla extricate, egg, and all-purpose flour until well combined.
3. Gradually pour the warm drain into the egg blend, whisking always to maintain a strategic distance from turning sour.
4. Pour the mixture back into the saucepan and return it to medium-low heat. Cook, stirring constantly, until the custard thickens and coats the back of a spoon (about 5 minutes). Remove it from the heat and let it cool.

<u>For the Pastry:</u>

1. Preheat your broiler to 350°F (175°C). Oil two little ramekins or ovenproof dishes.

2. Lay out one sheet of phyllo dough and brush it with melted butter. Place another sheet on top and brush it with more melted butter. Repeat with the remaining two sheets.
3. Cut the phyllo dough into two equal pieces.
4. Carefully line each greased ramekin with the layered phyllo dough, allowing any excess to hang over the edges.

To Assemble the Greek Syrup-Soaked Custard Pastry:

1. Spoon the cooled custard filling into each pastry-lined ramekin, spreading it evenly.
2. Fold the excess phyllo dough over the top of the custard to encase it.
3. If desired, sprinkle chopped walnuts or almonds for added texture and flavor.
4. Bake in the oven for 25-30 minutes or until the pastry is golden brown and crisp.

For the Syrup:

1. Whereas the baked goods are heating, get ready the syrup. Combine the granulated sugar, water, lemon juice, orange get-up-and-go (in case utilizing), ground cinnamon and vanilla extricate in a pot.
2. Bring the mixture to a boil, then reduce the heat and simmer for about 5 minutes or until it slightly thickens.
3. Expel the syrup from the warm and let it cool.

To Finish:

1. Once the cakes are done preparing, evacuate them from the stove and instantly pour the cooled syrup over them. Allow the pastries to absorb the syrup and cool for a few minutes before serving.
2. Serve the Greek Syrup-Soaked Custard Pastries warm or at room temperature. Enjoy this delightful Mediterranean dessert for two!

These syrup-soaked custard pastries are a delicious and sweet treat with a flaky phyllo crust, creamy custard filling, and fragrant syrup. Perfect for sharing with a loved one.

LEMON OLIVE OIL CAKE

Servings: 2
Prep Time: 15 minutes
Cook Time: 25-30 minutes

Nutrition Info (per serving):

- Calories: 380
- Protein: 4g
- Carbohydrates: 46g
- Dietary Fiber: 1g
- Sugars: 27g
- Fat: 21g
- Saturated Fat: 3g
- Cholesterol: 80mg
- Sodium: 180mg
- Potassium: 80mg

Ingredients:

- 1/2 cup all-purpose flour
- 1/4 teaspoon baking powder
- 1/8 teaspoon baking soda

- Pinch of salt
- Zest of 1 lemon
- 1/4 cup granulated sugar
- 1/4 cup extra-virgin olive oil
- 1/4 cup Greek yogurt (plain or vanilla)
- 1/2 teaspoon vanilla extract
- 1 large egg
- 1 tablespoon lemon juice (from the zested lemon)

For the Lemon Glaze:

- 1/4 cup powdered sugar
- 1 tablespoon lemon juice

Directions:

1. Preheat your oven to 350°F (175°C). Grease and flour two small ramekins or mini cake pans (about 4 inches in diameter).
2. Whisk together the all-purpose flour, baking powder, baking soda, and a pinch of salt in a small bowl. Set aside.
3. In another bowl, combine the lemon pizzazz and granulated sugar. Utilize your fingers to rub the magnetism into the sugar until it is fragrant.
4. Add the extra-virgin olive oil to the lemon sugar mixture and mix until well combined.
5. Mix within the Greek yogurt, vanilla extricate, and egg until smooth.
6. Gradually add the dry flour mixture to the wet mixture until just combined.
7. Finally, add the lemon juice and mix until incorporated.
8. Pour the cake player equitably into the arranged ramekins or smaller-than-expected cake container.
9. Heat within the stove for 25-30 minutes or until a toothpick embedded into the center comes clean.
10. While the cakes are baking, prepare the lemon glaze. Whisk together the powdered sugar and lemon juice in a small bowl until you have a smooth glaze.
11. Once the cakes are done baking, remove them from the oven and let them cool in the ramekins or pans for about 10 minutes.
12. Carefully modify the cakes onto a serving plate.
13. Drizzle the lemon glaze over the warm cakes.
14. Allow the Lemon Olive Oil Cakes to cool slightly before serving.
15. Serve the cakes as a delightful dessert for two. Enjoy the bright and citrusy flavors!

PALEO CHOCOLATE BANANA MUFFINS

Servings: 2
Prep Time: 10 minutes
Cook Time: 20-25 minutes

Nutrition Info (per serving):

- Calories: 300
- Protein: 6g
- Carbohydrates: 27g
- Dietary Fiber: 5g
- Sugars: 13g
- Fat: 20g
- Saturated Fat: 3g
- Cholesterol: 93mg
- Sodium: 190mg

- Potassium: 340mg

Ingredients:

- 1 ripe banana
- 2 large eggs
- 1/4 cup almond butter
- 2 tablespoons honey or maple syrup
- 1/4 cup almond flour
- 2 tablespoons coconut flour
- 2 tablespoons unsweetened cocoa powder
- 1/2 teaspoon baking powder
- 1/4 teaspoon baking soda
- Pinch of salt
- 1/4 cup dairy-free chocolate chips (optional)

Directions:

1. Preheat your oven to 350°F (175°C). Grease two muffin cups in a tin or line them with parchment paper liners.
2. In a mixing bowl, mash the ripe banana until smooth.
3. Add the eggs, almond butter, and honey (or maple syrup) to the mashed banana. Mix well until all the wet ingredients are combined.
4. Whisk together the almond flour, coconut flour, cocoa powder, planning powder, warming pop, and a press of salt in a separate bowl.
5. Gradually add the dry ingredients to the wet ingredients, mixing until you have a smooth batter.
6. If desired, fold in the dairy-free chocolate chips.
7. Divide the muffin batter evenly between the two prepared muffin cups.
8. Bake in the preheated oven for 20-25 minutes, or until a toothpick inserted into the center of a muffin comes out clean or with a few moist crumbs.
9. Remove the muffins from the oven and let them cool in the tin for a few minutes.
10. Exchange the biscuits on a wire rack to cool totally.
11. Once cooled, serve your Paleo Chocolate Banana Muffins as a delicious and nutritious treat for two.

DARK CHOCOLATE COVERED STRAWBERRIES

Servings: 2
Prep Time: 15 minutes
Chilling Time: 30 minutes

Nutrition Info (per serving):

- Calories: 150
- Protein: 1g
- Carbohydrates: 20g
- Dietary Fiber: 2g
- Sugars: 16g
- Fat: 8g
- Saturated Fat: 5g
- Cholesterol: 0mg
- Sodium: 0mg
- Potassium: 160mg

Ingredients:

- 12 fresh strawberries, rinsed and dried (with stems intact)

- 3 ounces (about 1/2 cup) dark chocolate chips or chunks (70% cocoa or higher)
- 1/2 teaspoon coconut oil (optional for smoother chocolate)
- Toppings (optional): Chopped nuts, shredded coconut, or sea salt flakes

Directions:

1. Line a preparing sheet or a huge plate with material paper. Once coated, this will be utilized to put the chocolate-covered strawberries.
2. Melt the dark chocolate chips or chunks in a microwave-safe bowl or double boiler. If using the microwave, heat the chocolate in 20-second intervals, stirring until it's fully melted. If using a twofold evaporator, soften the chocolate over stewing water, always blending.
3. If you'd like a smoother chocolate consistency, stir in the optional 1/2 teaspoon of coconut oil.
4. Holding a strawberry by the stem, dip it into the melted chocolate, swirling to coat about two-thirds of the strawberry. Allow any excess chocolate to drip off.
5. If you want to add toppings, sprinkle them over the chocolate-covered strawberry while it's still wet.
6. Place the chocolate-covered strawberry on the parchment-lined baking sheet or plate.
7. Repeat the dipping process with the remaining strawberries.
8. Once all the strawberries are coated, place the baking sheet or plate in the refrigerator for about 30 minutes or until the chocolate has fully hardened.
9. After chilling, the Dark Chocolate Covered Strawberries are ready to be served.
10. Enjoy your delicious and romantic treat for two!

CONCLUSION

Embrace a Lifelong Journey of Health and Flavor

Congratulations on embarking on the Mediterranean diet journey! By now, you've experienced the delightful flavors, nourishing ingredients, and numerous health benefits this diet offers. But the journey doesn't end here; it's just the beginning of a lifelong adventure in healthy living and culinary exploration.

Savor the Long-Term Benefits

One of the most remarkable aspects of the Mediterranean diet is its sustainability. Unlike restrictive diets that may leave you feeling deprived, the Mediterranean way of eating is a lifestyle that can be sustained over the long haul. It's not about quick fixes or drastic changes; it's about making mindful choices that enhance your well-being.

Nourish Your Body and Soul

As you continue to incorporate the principles of the Mediterranean diet into your daily life, you'll notice how it positively impacts your physical health and overall well-being. The abundance of fresh fruits and vegetables, heart-healthy fats, lean proteins, and whole grains nourishes your body, giving you energy and vitality. And the joy of savoring delicious, wholesome meals with loved ones can bring immense satisfaction and a sense of connection.

Cultivate Culinary Creativity

One of the joys of the Mediterranean diet is its versatility. The rich tapestry of Mediterranean cuisine offers endless ingredients, recipes, and flavors waiting to be explored. Don't hesitate to get creative in the kitchen, experimenting with new recipes and regional specialties. You'll discover a world of culinary treasures to keep your taste buds excited and engaged.

Make It Your Own

Remember that the Mediterranean diet is not a one-size-fits-all approach. It's a flexible framework tailored to your individual preferences and dietary needs. Whether you're a seafood enthusiast, a plant-based devotee, or somewhere in between, you can adapt this diet to suit your unique tastes and requirements.

Stay Mindful and Balanced

In your journey with the Mediterranean diet, balance and mindfulness are key. Continue to savor your meals slowly, enjoying each bite. Stay mindful of portion sizes and listen to your body's hunger and fullness cues. The main thing is to drink lots of water to stay hydrated and the occasional glass of red wine in moderation, if you choose.

Celebrate the Mediterranean Lifestyle

Finally, embrace the Mediterranean lifestyle beyond the plate. Incorporate physical activity, like brisk walks or dancing, into your routine. Spend time with people you love at the dinner table, sharing laughter and stories. Savor life's simple pleasures, like a sunny day, a good book, or a stroll by the sea.

Your Mediterranean Journey Continues

Your journey with the Mediterranean diet celebrates life, health, and the pleasures of good food. As you continue on this path, may you discover new culinary horizons, nourish your body and soul, and revel in the vibrant and flavorful world of Mediterranean cuisine. Cheers to your lifelong adventure in health and well-being!

Made in the USA
Las Vegas, NV
25 February 2024